Stability Analysis and Controller Design
of Local Model Networks

Christian Mayr

Stability Analysis and Controller Design of Local Model Networks

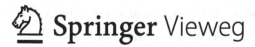 Springer Vieweg

Christian Mayr
IODP-XSA
AVL List GmbH
Graz, Austria

The financial support by the Austrian Federal Ministry for Digital and Economic Affairs, the National Foundation for Research, Technology and Development, the Christian Doppler Research Association and AVL List GmbH is gratefully acknowledged.

ISBN 978-3-658-34007-0   ISBN 978-3-658-34008-7   (eBook)
https://doi.org/10.1007/978-3-658-34008-7

Responsible Editor: Carina Reibold
This Springer Vieweg imprint is published by the registered company Springer Fachmedien Wiesbaden GmbH part of Springer Nature.
The registered company address is: Abraham-Lincoln-Str. 46, 65189 Wiesbaden, Germany

*For my wife Tamara
and my son Dominik
with all my love.*

Danksagung

Diese Dissertation entstand während meiner Beschäftigung als Projektassistent im Rahmen des Christian Doppler Labors für Modellbasierte Kalibriermethoden, am Institut für Mechanik und Mechatronik, Abteilung für Regelungstechnik und Prozessautomatisierung unter der Leitung von Univ. Prof. Dr. Stefan Jakubek. Insbesondere gilt mein Dank Dr. Stefan Jakubek, Dr. Martin Kozek und Dr. Christoph Hametner für die kompetente Betreuung. Durch ihre fachkundige Unterstützung wurde diese Arbeit erst möglich.

Dank geht auch an den Projektpartner AVL List GmbH. Neben der Finanzierung dieser Arbeit möchte ich mich bei den Mitarbeitern für die zahlreichen und interessanten Diskussionen bedanken, welche durch die hohen Ansprüche und ihre Ideen diese Arbeit wesentlich beeinflusst haben.

Weiters bedanke ich mich bei meinen Kollegen am Institut, die das gute Arbeitsklima wesentlich mitgestaltet haben und für fachliche Diskussionen jederzeit zur Verfügung standen.

Der größte Dank gilt jedoch meiner Frau Tamara für ihre Unterstützung und ihr Verständnis für die Arbeit. An dieser Stelle möchte ich mich noch bei meinen Eltern bedanken, welche mir meine Ausbildung ermöglicht haben und mich jederzeit unterstützt haben.

Christian Mayr

Kurzfassung

Die Forderung nach einer Reduktion der Entwicklungskosten und des CO_2 Ausstoßes von Kraftfahrzeugen sowie immer strenger werdende Abgasnormen führen in der Automobilindustrie zu einer steigenden Nachfrage nach modellbasierten Kalibriermethoden. In diesem Zusammenhang sind lokale Modellnetzwerke ein sehr leistungsstarkes Instrument zur nichtlinearen dynamischen Identifikation. Ihre generische Modellstruktur ist besonders dann von Vorteil, wenn physikalische Informationen des nichtlinearen Prozesses eingebracht werden können. Dadurch, dass diese Systemarchitektur das nichtlineare Systemverhalten mittels lokaler linearer Übertragungsfunktionen approximiert, sind lokale Modellnetzwerke, im Vergleich zu anderen nichtlinearen Approximatoren, wie z. B.: Neuronale Netze oder Radiale Basisfunktionen, sehr gut für die Reglerauslegung geeignet. Der größte Vorteil besteht darin, dass, zumindest auf lokaler Ebene, lineare Methoden zur Reglerauslegung verwendet werden können. Die lokale Auslegung erweist sich dabei in der Regel als gute Ausgangsbasis für die globale, nichtlineare Auslegung.

In dieser Dissertation werden verschiedene Methoden zur Stabilitätsanalyse und Reglerauslegung von lokalen Modellnetzwerken dargestellt. Für die praktische Verwendung von lokalen Modellnetzwerken spielt die Stabilität eine besonders wichtige Rolle. Die Untersuchung der Stabilität von lokalen Modellnetzwerken basiert auf der direkten Methode nach Lyapunov. Aus deren Stabilitätsbedingungen resultieren für lokale Modellnetzwerke sogenannte LMIs (Linear Matrix Inequalities) welche numerisch gelöst werden. Hier spielt die Konservativität eine entscheidende Rolle, da ein Stabilitätsnachweis, je nach verwendeter Lyapunov Funktion, scheitern kann obwohl das System stabil ist. Es wurden drei verschiedene Ansätze untersucht und weiterentwickelt sowie Methoden entwickelt um deren Konservativität zu verringern und quantitativ messbar zu machen.

Ein weiterer wichtiger Teil dieser Dissertation sind die Stabilitätskriterien für den geschlossenen Regelkreis. Diese verwenden dieselben Lyapunov Funktionen wie die Kriterien für den offenen Regelkreis. Mit diesen Ansätzen ist es möglich, bestehende Regler-Strecken Kombinationen auf Stabilität zu prüfen. Eine direkte Auslegung von Reglern mit garantierter Stabilität des geschlossenen Regelkreises ist mit diesen Kriterien nicht möglich. Es ist allerdings möglich diese Kriterien zu adaptieren bzw. mit nichtlinearer Optimierung zu kombinieren um stabile State-Feedback sowie PID Regler auszulegen. Hier spielt die impliziete Konservativität des Lyapunov Ansatzes ebenfalls eine entscheidende Rolle, da es auch hier vorkommen kann, dass ein Stabilitätsnachweis scheitert, obwohl der geschlossene Regelkreis stabil ist.

Die Auslegung von stabilen State-Feedback Reglern für lokale Modellnetzwerke basiert auf den Stabilitätskriterien des geschlossenen Regelkreises. Durch auftretende Matrixmultiplikationen zwischen den lokalen Rückführmatrizen und der Matrix bzw. den Matrizen der Lyapunov Funktion entstehen sogenannte BMIs (**B**ilinear **M**atrix **I**nequalities) die von LMI Solvern nicht gelöst werden können. Durch eine Matrixtransformation innerhalb der Matrixungleichungen ist es möglich, die BMIs in LMIs umzuwandeln, die wiederum einfach von LMI Solvern gelöst werden können.

Der letzte Hauptteil dieser Arbeit beschäftigt sich mit der PID Reglerauslegung für lokale Modellnetzwerke. Bei nichtlinearen PID Reglern für lokale Modellnetzwerke ist der Stabilitätsnachweis bzw. die Auslegung wesentlich aufwändiger als bei Zustandsreglern. Dabei ist eine Transformation des geschlossenen Regelkreises (LMN & PID Regler) erforderlich. Die größte Herausforderung besteht jedoch bei der Reglerauslegung. Durch die begrenzte Anzahl der Reglerparameter ist die Transformation der BMIs in LMIs, wie es bei Zustandsraumreglern der Fall ist, nicht mehr möglich. Daher können die Matrixungleichungen bei PID Reglern nicht mit Hilfe von LMI Solvern gelöst werden. Die Weiterentwicklung der ersten Solver für BMIs wurde mittlerweile wieder eingestellt und derzeit ist kein brauchbarer Solver verfügbar. Daher werden in dieser Arbeit zwei Lösungsansätze vorgestellt. Beim ersten wird iterativ gearbeitet wobei in jedem Iterationsschritt LMIs zu lösen sind. Bei der zweiten Methode wird ein genetischer Algorithmus für die Festlegung der PID Reglerparameter verwendet wobei für jedes Individuum die LMIs gelöst werden müssen, was einen sehr hohen Rechenaufwand darstellt. Der genetische Algorithmus lässt sich allerdings sehr gut parallelisieren wodurch beim Einsatz von modernen Mehrkernprozessoren der Zeitaufwand in Grenzen gehalten werden kann. Im Allgemeinen hat sich dieser Ansatz als sehr leistungsstark erwiesen und zeigt eine gute Konvergenz. Des Weiteren ermöglicht der genetische Algorithmus die simultane Optimierung von (gegensätzlichen) Optimierungskriterien. Daher wurde dieser Ansatz erweitert, um Stabilität und Performance des geschlossenen Regelkreises in der Optimierung zu berücksichtigen. Der Anwender erhält mehrere gleichwertige Lösungen zur Auswahl. Theoretisch kann dieser Ansatz auch für State-Feedback Regler verwendet werden, was allerdings nicht im Fokus dieser Arbeit stand.

Zusätzlich gibt es einen kurzen Überblick über die Vor- und Nachteile der verbreitetsten LMI Solver.

Abstract

In automotive applications more and more stringent emission regulations and the desire to reduce fuel consumption lead to an increasing demand for efficient and reliable modeling tools. In this context local models have proved to be a powerful tool in nonlinear dynamic system identification. Their generic nonlinear model representation is particularly useful if information about the structure of the nonlinearity is available, [1]. Local model networks (LMNs) approximated the nonlinear system dynamics by means of locally linear transfer functions. Thus, this system architecture is more suitable for controller design compared to alternative approximation methods, e.g. neural networks or radial basis function networks. The main advantage is that linear controller design methods can be, at least locally, applied. Such a local calibration is commonly a good basis for a global, nonlinear controller calibration method.

This thesis treats various methods for stability analysis and controller design of LMNs. For the practical application of LMNs stability is of major interest. Stability analysis of LMNs is based on Lyapunov's direct method. From the stability condition follow LMIs (Linear Matrix Inequalities) which are numerically solved. In this context the conservatism is crucial because a stability proof may fail even when the system is globally stable, depending on the used Lyapunov criterion. For this purpose, three commonly used Lyapunov approaches were extended to reduce their conservatism and provide a quantitative measure for their comparison.

A further important part of this thesis are stability criteria of the closed loop. These approaches use the same Lyapunov function as the criteria for the open loop. With these criteria it is possible to analyze stability of existing controller-plant combinations, but direct controller calibration with guaranteed stability is not possible. Nevertheless, it is possible to adapt these criteria or combine them with nonlinear optimization to calibrate stable state-feedback as well as PID controller. As for open loop stability analysis the conservatism is crucial, because it may happen that a stability proof is not possible although the closed loop is globally stable.

The calibration of stable state-feedback controllers is based on the closed loop stability analysis methods. Here, so called BMIs (**B**ilinear **M**atrix **I**nequalities) arise because of occurrent matrix multiplications between the local feedback matrices and the matrices/matrix of the Lyapunov function. For state-feedback controllers a matrix transformation within the matrix inequalities allows the transformation from BMIs (**B**ilinear **M**atrix **I**nequalities) to LMIs, which can be solved by LMI solvers.

The last main part of this thesis treats PID controller design for LMNs. The calibration of nonlinear PID controllers for LMNs is significantly more complex than the calibration of state-feedback controllers. The required transformation of the closed loop (LMN & PID controller) into a state-space model is significantly more advanced than for state-feedback controller. However, the main challenge lies in the controller calibration. The mentioned matrix transformation from BMIs into LMIs is not possible and thus not solvable for LMI solvers. Currently, the development of the first BMI solver is discontinued and no useful BMI solver is available. Thus, two approaches are treated in this work. The first approach works iteratively to get LMIs in each iteration step. The second approach uses a genetic algorithm to determine the PID controller parameters where for each individual the stability is checked, which results in a high calculation effort. The results have shown, that this approach is powerful and has a good convergency. Further, the genetic algorithm allows simultaneous enhancement of (competing) optimization criteria. Thus, this approach was extended to evaluate stability and performance of the closed loop. A calibration engineer can choose between multiple equivalent results. Theoretically, this approach can be adopted for state-feedback controllers, but this was not focus of this work.

Contents

List of Figures

List of Tables

Introduction 1

1.1 Motivation

In recent years model-based calibration has become more important in many industrial fields. In automotive industry calibration is known as the optimal parameterization of various controller parameters for vehicles, engines and their subsystems. Typical calibration tasks aim at performance and stability of the closed loop. For combustion engines common examples for calibration tasks are breathing controls for the air path and the spark angle. For hybrid vehicles a typical example is the optimization of the hybrid control unit (HCU) which manages the energy flow and aims at minimal fuel consumption. Such optimization tasks have to find a compromise between competing objectives and are thus multi-objective.

Regarding stronger emission legislations and due to the desire to reduce the fuel consumption an increasing demand on methodologies for testing and optimizing internal combustion engines is quested in automotive applications. Generally, the overall efficiency demand impacts the modern engine and powertrain development processes: Computationally powerful engine control units (ECUs) and the application of new sensors enable new and more effective control strategies on the one hand. On the other hand the reduction of development costs and the requirements for the automotive industry regarding emission norms are continuously tightened. Due to the fact that engine testbed operations involve excessive costs, the goal is to optimize the trade-off between quality, timing and costs.

The optimization of various controller parameters for both feedforward and feedback controllers in control units for combustion engines and vehicles aims the following (conflicting) goals: Fuel consumption, legal emission standards, subjective drivability, measurable vehicle performance, on-board diagnosis (OBD) requirements. In ECUs usually discrete-time, nonlinear PID controllers with a specific

© The Author(s), under exclusive license to Springer Fachmedien Wiesbaden GmbH, part of Springer Nature 2021
C. Mayr, *Stability Analysis and Controller Design of Local Model Networks*,
https://doi.org/10.1007/978-3-658-34008-7_1

structure are used for many control tasks (e.g. turbocharger position for intake manifold pressure control). Basically, the nonlinear PID gains are maps which depend on engine load and speed. Further, there are additional parameters to distinguish between small and large control errors. Usually calibration engineers determine the parameters and maps within the ECU structure using testbed runs, test drives and a lot of expert knowledge. Due to the complex controller structure and the nonlinear process model-based approaches are suitable for controller calibration tasks. In this context it is common to use local linearizations which make the design of controllers for nonlinear systems easier or even possible. In previous works LMNs from the family of multiple-model approaches have shown that they are a qualified approach for data driven local linearizations with superior global nonlinear approximation capabilities at the same time. LMN interpolate between different local models, each valid in a certain operating regime which represents a simple model, e.g. a linear regression model. One important advantage of LMN is that their inherent definitions of operating regimes can be adopted to schedule the controller parameters or generate parameter maps. Due to the local approximation with linear systems it is possible to develop methods which are based on linear methods. It is noteworthy that just using linear methods and schedule the resulting controller parameters may lead to globally unstable and/or bad performing nonlinear controllers. Thus, it is necessary to involve closed loop stability analysis for nonlinear systems within controller design methods. To sum up, current and upcoming emission and fuel efficiency limitations will make it necessary to unleash the full potential of modern combustion engines by using the most sophisticated computer aided calibration and optimization methods.

1.2   Main Goals

In the course of this work stability analysis- and controller design methods are developed for nonlinear systems, represented by LMNs. Existing methodologies for open loop stability as well as design and stability analysis of control systems based on LMNs are investigated and extended. The main advantage of using a model-based controller design approach lies in the fact that the task can be accomplished by using the LMN instead of the physical process. However, the architecture of LMNs also provides the ability of designing and analyzing controllers based on local linear models and analyzing stability and performance of the nonlinear control loop based on the global nonlinear model virtually at the same time. Thus, LMNs provide a basis to analyze and evaluate many generally accepted industrial nonlinear control system designs such as gain scheduling control. Additionally this work aims at the applicability of LMN based stability analysis and controller design methods on real-world problems, especially to the specific demands in the automotive industry. The main goals of this work were, [5]:

- To analyze and extend *open loop stability analysis methods* for a system represented by an LMN. This involves existing stability conditions from literature as well as their enhancement for application in complex real systems.
- To evaluate and enhance *closed loop stability conditions* for an LMN with a *pre-existing* controller.
- To support the *design of controllers* based on an existing local model network (e.g. a gain-scheduled controller).

Dynamic Local Model Networks

2

2.1 Introduction

LMNs are a well-established multiple-model approach, e.g. [6, 7, 8, 9], for nonlinear dynamic system identification. These model architectures interpolate between different local models, each valid in a certain operating regime which offers a versatile structure for the identification of nonlinear static and dynamic systems, [9]. Each operating regime represents a simple model, e.g. a linear regression model, where the local dynamics are usually defined as transfer functions. There exist many methods for the identification of nonlinear systems by means of LMNs, e.g. [7, 9, 10, 11, 12, 13]. Due to the increased transparency of the LMN structure the incorporation of prior (physical) knowledge is easily possible, [9]. Another widely-used model architecture are Takagi Sugeno (TS) fuzzy models, e.g. [14]. The similarity between the TS and LMN models can be easily noticed if the number of fuzzy if-then rules in the TS model equals the number of local models in an LMN, [15]. In comparison to radial basis function networks (RBFN) (e.g. [16]) the local models in an LMN are active over a larger subspace and consequently, the number of local models can be reduced dramatically, [15]. Nevertheless, when LMNs approximate a physical process they may comprise many local models, use a complex partitioning strategy, have a high dimensional partition space or strongly nonlinear dynamics. Furthermore, there is no unique LMN to approximate a particular process. Different LMNs may lead to comparable results by using different parameters and structures (number of local models, partitioning strategy, regularization, identification method).

© The Author(s), under exclusive license to Springer Fachmedien Wiesbaden GmbH, part of Springer Nature 2021
C. Mayr, *Stability Analysis and Controller Design of Local Model Networks*, https://doi.org/10.1007/978-3-658-34008-7_2

2.2   Architecture of Dynamic Local Model Networks

The architecture of dynamic LMNs is depicted in Figure 2.1.

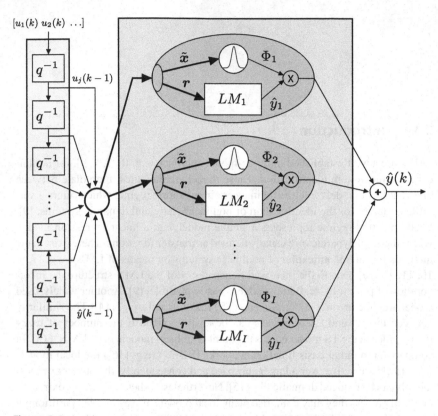

Figure 2.1 Architecture of a multiple input single output (MISO) LMN with external dynamics [17]; u_i: inputs, $\hat{y}$: global output, $\hat{y}_i$: local outputs, r: regression vector, $\tilde{x}$: partition vector, Φ_i: validity functions, q^{-1}: shift operator

First, an ordered set for the indices of the local models is defined:

$$\mathcal{I} = (i \in \mathbb{N} | 1 \leq i \leq I) \tag{2.1}$$

where I denotes the number of local linear models. LMNs with external dynamics have an input vector $r(k)$, usually called regressor, with past inputs and outputs according to Figure 2.1:

$$r(k) = \left[u_{\mathcal{J}}(k - \mathcal{M}_{\mathcal{J}})\, \hat{y}(k - \mathcal{N})\ 1 \right], \quad r(k) \in \mathbb{R}^{1 \times O} \tag{2.2}$$

where O denotes the dimension of the input vector. The ordered sets for the number of the input channels $\mathcal{J}$ and the indices of the input vector $\mathcal{O}$ are defined as follows:

$$\mathcal{J} = (j \in \mathbb{N} | 1 \le j \le J) \tag{2.3}$$
$$\mathcal{O} = (o \in \mathbb{N} | 1 \le o \le O), \tag{2.4}$$

where J denotes the number of inputs. The sets for the order of the used time delays of the inputs $\mathcal{M}_{\mathcal{J}}$ and the feedback output (= system order) $\mathcal{N}$ may be user defined:

$$m_{\mathcal{J}} \in \mathcal{M}_{\mathcal{J}}, \quad M_{\mathcal{J}} = \max(\mathcal{M}_{\mathcal{J}}), \quad \forall \mathcal{J} \tag{2.5}$$
$$n \in \mathcal{N}, \quad N = \max(\mathcal{N}) \tag{2.6}$$

where $\mathcal{M}_{\mathcal{J}}$ denotes the numerator orders of the inputs, $m_{\mathcal{J}}$ denotes the number of elements of $\mathcal{M}_{\mathcal{J}}$, N denotes the system order and n denotes the number of elements of $\mathcal{N}$. From Figure 2.1 it becomes obvious that the input vector of the validity functions $\Phi_{\mathcal{I}}(\tilde{x}(k))$, which is defined in the so-called partition space, can be chosen differently to the input vector of the local models:

$$\tilde{x}(k) = \left[u_{\tilde{\mathcal{J}}}(k - \tilde{\mathcal{M}}_{\tilde{\mathcal{J}}})\, \hat{y}(k - \tilde{\mathcal{N}}) \right], \quad \tilde{x}(k) \in \mathbb{R}^{1 \times \tilde{O}} \tag{2.7}$$

where the ordered sets $\tilde{\mathcal{J}}$ and $\tilde{\mathcal{O}}$ are subsets of their corresponding sets as follows:

$$\tilde{\mathcal{J}} \subseteq \mathcal{J} \tag{2.8}$$
$$\tilde{\mathcal{O}} \subseteq \mathcal{O}, \tag{2.9}$$

and the sets $\tilde{\mathcal{M}}_{\tilde{\mathcal{J}}}, \tilde{\mathcal{N}}$ are defined equivalent to (2.5) and (2.6),

$$\tilde{m}_{\tilde{\mathcal{J}}} \in \tilde{\mathcal{M}}_{\tilde{\mathcal{J}}}, \forall \mathcal{J} \tag{2.10}$$
$$\tilde{n} \in \tilde{\mathcal{N}}. \tag{2.11}$$

There are several partitioning strategies for LMNs. Figure 2.2 illustrates six common strategies.

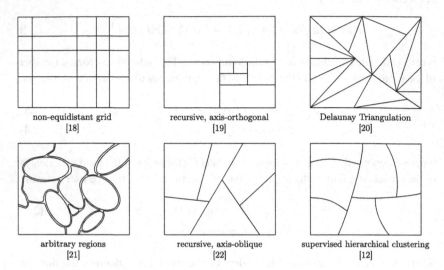

Figure 2.2 Common partitioning strategies of LMNs

Furthermore, three different types of validity functions are commonly used, see Figure 2.3.

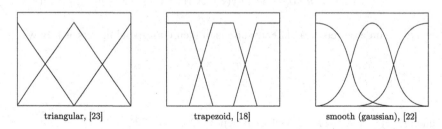

Figure 2.3 Common validity functions of LMNs

The local model outputs

$$\hat{y}_i(k) = r(k)\theta_i, \quad \forall \mathcal{I} \tag{2.12}$$

with the local parameter vector

$$\theta_i = \left[b_{\mathcal{J}.\mathcal{M}_\mathcal{J}}^{(i)} \ a_\mathcal{N}^{(i)} \ c^{(i)} \right]^T, \quad \theta_i \in \mathbb{R}^{O \times 1}, \quad \forall \mathcal{I} \tag{2.13}$$

are used subsequently to form the global model output $\hat{y}(k)$ by weighted aggregation, see Figure 2.1:

$$\hat{y}(k) = \sum_{\mathcal{I}} \Phi_i(\tilde{x}(k))\hat{y}_i(k), \tag{2.14}$$

where the validity functions are constrained to form a partition of unity:

$$\sum_{\mathcal{I}} \Phi_i = 1 \tag{2.15}$$

$$0 \le \Phi_i \le 1, \quad \forall \mathcal{I}. \tag{2.16}$$

The notation of the parameters by using sets is described by means of a short example:

Example 2.1 *Assume that the LMN has two inputs $\mathcal{J} = (1, 2)$ where the inputs use the following orders $\mathcal{M}_1 = \{1, 3\}$, $\mathcal{M}_2 = \{2, 4\}$ and the used order of the output is $\mathcal{N} = \{1, 2, 4\}$. The parameter vector (2.13) is defined as follows:*

$$\theta_i = \left[b_{1.1}^{(i)} \ b_{1.3}^{(i)} \ b_{2.2}^{(i)} \ b_{2.4}^{(i)} \ a_1^{(i)} \ a_2^{(i)} \ a_4^{(i)} \ c^{(i)} \right]^T$$

The global model output $\hat{y}(k)$ can be reformulated as a parameter varying discrete-time transfer function:

$$\hat{y}(k) = \sum_{\mathcal{I}} \Phi_i(\tilde{x}(k)) \cdot \frac{\sum_{\mathcal{J}} u_j(k) \cdot \left(\sum_{\mathcal{M}_j} b_{j.m_j}^{(i)} \cdot q^{-m} \right) + c^{(i)}}{1 - \sum_{\mathcal{I}} \Phi_i(\tilde{x}(k)) \cdot \sum_{\mathcal{N}} a_n^{(i)} \cdot q^{-n}} \tag{2.17}$$

2.3   Review of the Hierarchical Discriminant Tree, [2, 3]

The method performs a recursive partitioning of the partition space, [9]. In each iteration step a new local linear model is added to the model tree by splitting the worst local model. Related to [24] the growing tree can be described by a binary tree where each node corresponds to a split of the partition space into two parts. Fig. 2.4 shows the hierarchical tree used for the computation of the membership functions Φ_i, [25], [26]. Each node represents a discriminant function $\varphi(\tilde{x})$, $R^p \rightarrow R$. The free ends of the branches represent the actual local models with their validity functions Φ_i and the parameter vectors θ_i.

Figure 2.4 Hierarchical discriminant tree, [9]

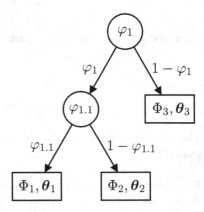

The validity functions for the layout in Fig. 2.4 are obtained by

$$\Phi_1 = \varphi_1 \varphi_{1.1}, \tag{2.18}$$

$$\Phi_2 = \varphi_1(1 - \varphi_{1.1}), \tag{2.19}$$

$$\Phi_3 = 1 - \varphi_1. \tag{2.20}$$

The main advantage of this choice is that a partition of unity throughout the partition space is guaranteed and no normalisation side effects like reactivations can occur.

In each iteration step the worst local model of the growing tree is replaced by a new node and two new models. The partitioning is obtained considering a two-category classification problem. According to [27] the nonlinear discriminant function for the two classes is given by the logistic sigmoid activation function (Fig. 2.5):

Figure 2.5 Logistic sigmoid activation function, [22]

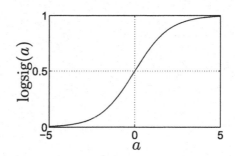

$$\varphi(\tilde{x}(k)) = \frac{1}{1 + \exp(-a(\tilde{x}(k)))} \tag{2.21}$$

with

$$a(\tilde{x}(k)) = \begin{bmatrix} 1 & \tilde{x}^T(k) \end{bmatrix} \begin{bmatrix} \psi_0 \\ \tilde{\psi} \end{bmatrix}. \tag{2.22}$$

Figure 2.6 Linear decision boundary of the nonlinear discriminant function, [2]

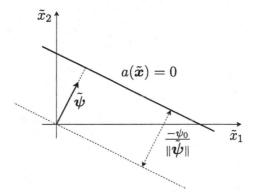

Here, $\tilde{\psi}^T = \begin{bmatrix} \psi_1 \dots \psi_p \end{bmatrix}$ denotes the weight vector and ψ_0 is called bias term. Accordingly weight vector and bias term are collected in the augmented weight vector

$$\psi^T = \begin{bmatrix} \psi_0 & \psi_1 \dots \psi_p \end{bmatrix}. \tag{2.23}$$

Since the input argument in (2.21) is linear in its input $\tilde{x}(k)$ the decision boundary is also linear in the partition space (Fig. 2.6).

Open Loop Stability Analysis   3

3.1   Introduction

When LMNs are constructed from measured input and output data only, they constitute a special approach to nonlinear system identification. Whenever such LMNs are used for sensitive or critical purposes such as hardware in the loop simulation or control design the question of stability analysis naturally arises. Basically, a dynamic LMN may become globally unstable even if its local submodels are stable, [18]. For nonlinear systems stability is preferably checked by Lyapunov's direct method, [28]. For LMNs Lyapunov based stability criteria can be adopted from Takagi Sugeno (TS) fuzzy models, e.g. [29, 30, 31, 32, 33, 34, 35, 36, 37, 38, 39, 40, 41, 42] which usually result in linear matrix inequalities (LMIs). The adoption of these methods is justified if the number of fuzzy if-then rules in the TS model equals the number of local models in an LMN, [15]. Nevertheless, when LMNs approximate a physical process they may be much more complex than usual TS fuzzy models. In general, Lyapunov based stability criteria provide *sufficient* rather than necessary conditions. In this context the issue of *conservatism* is inherently linked to these methods.

This chapter makes two contributions for Lyapunov stability analysis of LMNs: The first method provides the ability to quantify the conservatism of different Lyapunov approaches. The basic idea is to use the achievable decay rate of different Lyapunov stability criteria. Due to the conservatism of Lyapunov stability criteria the achievable decay rates will be different than the decay rate of the actual system. Thus, different criteria will result in different maximum decay rates for the

Electronic supplementary material The online version of this chapter (https://doi.org/10.1007/978-3-658-34008-7_3) contains supplementary material, which is available to authorized users.

same system. In contrast to existing approaches (e.g. [31]) where the decay rate is a constant parameter, the decay rate is defnined as an additional decision variable for the LMI solver. The main advantage of this approach is that the *extremal* decay rate and the LMIs can be solved *simultaneously* by a suitable optimization method. In contrast, a common method to compare the conservatism of different Lyapunov approaches is to use, usually 2-dimensional, parameter spaces (e.g. [36, 43]). Within this parameter space two selected system parameters are varied for a point-wise analysis of the provable stability region for different Lyapunov approaches. The main issue of such an approach is the limited informative value for high dimensional systems. The proposed method is designed for the workflow of system identification—the informative value of the conservatism assertion is independent of the dimension of the system and the system parameters need not to be varied.

In this chapter three Lyapunov approaches are considered which are based on TS fuzzy systems:

- The *Common Quadratic Lyapunov approach* [18] which aims to find a single quadratic Lyapunov function for all local linear models in an LMN.
- The *Piecewise Quadratic Lyapunov approach* [30] which aims to find connected local quadratic Lyapunov functions for the local linear models.
- The *Fuzzy Lyapunov approach* [34] which aims to find a global nonlinear Lyapunov function which is a weighted aggregation of local ones.

Both, in the piecewise quadratic- and the fuzzy Lyapunov approach the local Lyapunov functions are connected by so-called model transitions. They occur when the system state transits from one local model to another. The number of model transitions adversely increases the conservatism of these stability criteria. Thus, a reduction of the model transitions to those actually possible will help to improve these two approaches because impossible transitions need not be considered. Thus, the methodology presented in Section 3.5 aims at reducing the number of feasible transitions to a minimum. The basic idea is to capture the model transitions by means of the identification data sequence, [44].

For systems where the output is not a dimension of the partition space an eigenvalue analysis is sufficient to prove stability of LMNs which is discussed in Section 3.3.

3.2   Concepts of Stability, [4]

An autonomous dynamic system in discrete-time is represented by a set of difference
equations in the form

$$x(k+1) = f(x(k)), \; f \in \mathbb{R}^{n \times 1} \tag{3.1}$$

where f is a nonlinear vector function, x is the $n \times 1$ state vector, and k denotes the
sampling instant.

For nonlinear systems a number of refined stability concepts, such as marginal
stability and asymptotic stability are needed:

Definition 3.1 *An equilibrium state x^e is* marginally stable *if for every neighborhood $U > 0$ of x^e there is a neighborhood $T > 0$, $T \subseteq U$ of x^e such that every trajectory $x(k)$ starting within T ($x(0) \in T$) remains within U for all $k > 0$ (Figure 3.1, dashed line). Otherwise the equilibrium point x^e is* unstable *(Figure 3.1, dotted line).*

Note that $x(k)$ needs not approach x^e.

Definition 3.2 *An equilibrium state x^e is* asymptotically stable *(Figure 3.1, dash-dotted line) if it is marginal stable and additionally T can be chosen so that $\|x(k) - x^e\| \to 0$ as $k \to \infty$ for all $x(0) \in T$.*

The following defninition of exponential stability was adopted from [45]:

Definition 3.3 *A discrete-time system is said to be* globally exponentially stable *if there exist positive constants α, $0 < \alpha < 1$ and $\beta > 0$, such that*

$$\|x(k)\| \leq \alpha^k \beta \|x(0)\|, \; \forall k \in \mathbb{N}^+ \tag{3.2}$$

The number α is known as the decay rate.

Remark 3.1 *defninition 3.3 is analogous to the defninition of the decay rate in [31].*

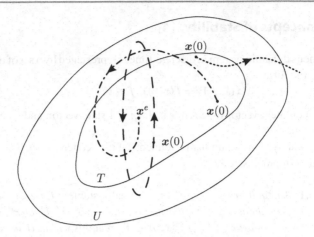

Figure 3.1 Stability defninitions, [4]

3.3   Open Loop Stability Analysis using Eigenvalue Analysis

LMNs where the partition space does not contain past system outputs are linear for constant inputs. Thus, a prerequisite for valid stability assertion using the method of this section is that the set for the elements of the system output in the partition space must be empty:

$$\hat{\mathcal{N}} = \{\} \tag{3.3}$$

When open loop stability of such LMNs is investigated it is sufficient to analyze the eigenvalue set. The denominator of an LMN's transfer function, see (2.17), defines the space where the poles or eigenvalues of the system may come to lie:

$$1 - \sum_{\mathcal{I}} \Phi_i(\tilde{x}) \cdot \sum_{\mathcal{N}} a_n^{(i)} \cdot q^{-n} = 0, \ \forall \hat{x} \tag{3.4}$$

The linear parameter interpolation by means of $\hat{x}$ may result in a strongly nonlinear interpolation behavior of (3.4). Thus, an interpolated system may become unstable even if the local systems are both stable and of order greater than two, [10].

For the sake of generality it is not sufficient to consider each possible $\hat{x}$. It is reasonable to determine the hull, which is in general not convex, of the eigenvalue space. For this purpose, the eigenvalues of the interpolation between two local models are considered because they bound the eigenvalue space:

$$A_1(q) = 1 - \Phi_1 \cdot \sum_{\mathcal{N}} a_n^{(1)} \cdot q^{-n}, \; A_2(q) = 1 - \Phi_2 \cdot \sum_{\mathcal{N}} a_n^{(2)} \cdot q^{-n} \qquad (3.5)$$

According to (3.4) the equation for the eigenvalue trace is as follows:

$$\Phi_1 A_1(q) y(q) + \Phi_2 A_2(q) y(q) = 0$$
$$\left(1 + \frac{\Phi_2}{\Phi_1} \frac{A_2(q)}{A_1(q)}\right) y(q) = 0 \qquad (3.6)$$

where the two considered local models must satisfy (2.15) and (2.16). From (3.6) it becomes obvious, that the eigenvalue trace between two local models is quite similar to root loci. Thus, because (3.6) must be satisfied for all $y(q)$ the following condition follows to guarantee global stability of an LMN which satisfies (3.3):

$$K \frac{A_2(q)}{A_1(q)} = -1 \qquad (3.7)$$

with

$$K = \frac{\Phi_2}{\Phi_1}, \quad \Phi_1 + \Phi_2 = 1 \;\rightarrow\; 0 \le K \le \infty.$$

In Figure 3.2(b) a stable and an unstable LMN are depicted. The colored lines represent an interpolation between two local models and the hull of all lines define the space where the eigenvalues of the LMN may come to lie. Thus, it is obvious

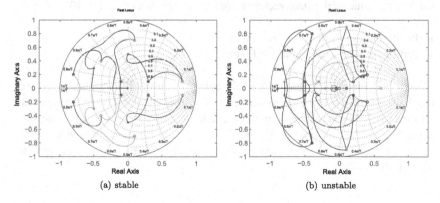

(a) stable   (b) unstable

Figure 3.2 Comparison of a stable and an unstable LMN

that for Figure 3.2(b) (3.7) is not satisfied and the LMN may become unstable in some interpolation regions and is not globally stable. In contrast to Figure 3.2(b) (3.7) is satisfied and thus the LMN is globally stable.

3.4   Open Loop Stability Analysis using Lyapunov's Direct Method

3.4.1   A Simple Motivating Example

For LMN or fuzzy systems a natural question arises of whether the global system is stable if all its local systems (all A_i) are stable. The answer is no in general, as illustrated by the following example, [46].

The investigated system consists of two locally stable linear subsystems with a trapezoid interpolation:

$$x(k+1) = \sum_{i=1}^{2} \Phi_i A_i x(k) \tag{3.8}$$

$$y = c^T x$$

with

$$A_1 = \begin{bmatrix} 1 & -0.5 \\ 1 & 0 \end{bmatrix}, \quad A_2 = \begin{bmatrix} -1 & -0.5 \\ 1 & 0 \end{bmatrix}, \quad c^T = \begin{bmatrix} 1 & 0 \end{bmatrix}, \quad x = \begin{bmatrix} x_1 \\ x_2 \end{bmatrix}$$

In the following two systems with different partitioning directions are compared, where the width of the interpolation regime is equal in both cases ($[-1\ 1]$). Further, the starting value of the state vector is equal for both cases ($x_0 = [10\ 10]^T$):

- Partitioning in x_1 direction, see Figure 3.3
- Partitioning in x_2 direction, see Figure 3.4

Thus, it is demonstrated that the global stability of an LMN not only depends on the dynamics of the linear subsystems. For this example it is not possible to find a Lyapunov function using common criteria because the system may be unstable, depending on the partitioning. Further, it shows the inherent conservatism of the Lyapunov approach because there exist partitioning directions where the system seems to be stable.

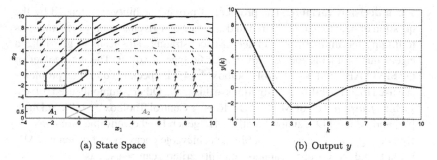

(a) State Space   (b) Output y

Figure 3.3 Partitioning in x_1: (seems to be) stable

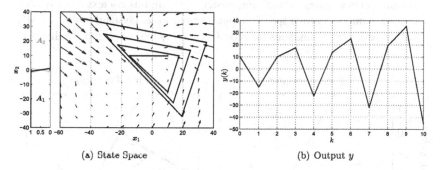

(a) State Space   (b) Output y

Figure 3.4 Partitioning in x_2: unstable

3.4.2   General

As shown in Section 3.4.1 an LMN with a state dependent partition space may
become unstable even when all local eigenvalues are stable. Thus, Section 3.4 treats
the conservatism of stability analysis using the common, the piecewise quadratic
and the fuzzy Lyapunov approach which are extended by the decay rate α. Basically,
the decay rate is an important characteristic of the dynamic behavior of a nonlinear
system. It provides the ability to prove exponential stability on the one hand and
comparability of different Lyapunov approaches on the other hand, [31]. In this
context two cases must be distinguished:

- α **is a constant:** This case is analogous to the existing approaches and not the
  focus of this paper. Exponential stability with a desired decay rate can be investigated instead of the asymptotic stability of the existing approaches.

- α **is a decision variable:** The problem of proving stability is extended by the question of how to find the extremal decay rate of a given system which amounts to finding the infimum of α under LMI constraints. This leads to generalized eigenvalue problems and requires a specific type of solver. The *gevp* solver of the MATLAB® Robust Control Toolbox™ [47] is specialized in such problems and used for all stability investigations in this work. Other commonly used solvers such as *feasp, mincx* of MATLAB® Robust Control Toolbox™ [47], SeDuMi [48] and Sdpt-3 [49] cannot directly solve generalized eigenvalue problems.

By treating α as a decision variable the achievable decay rate of different LMN variants and the various Lyapunov stability criteria can be used as a quantitative measure because different LMN variants or stability criteria will yield different maximum decay rates for the same system, [31]. In this context it is essential to keep in mind that for a specific input-output data set (system) arbitrary LMN variants exist and boundaries for provable stability may exist, too. To illustrate

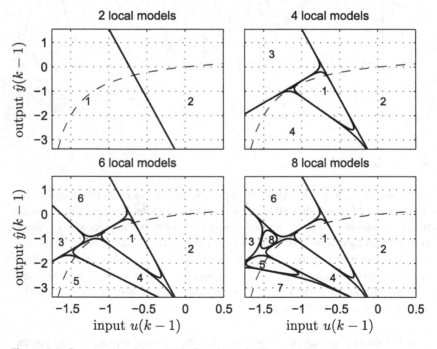

Figure 3.5 Contour plot of the validity functions of different LMN variants

this situation consider the example in Figure 3.5: Here, data from a nonlinear dynamic process are modeled by four different LMN variants.

One important bound is the maximum number of local models where a stability proof is still possible. This number is of particular interest because the approximation quality is usually increased by the number of local models whereas a proof of stability becomes increasingly difficult as the number of local models grows, [29]. Thus, it is possible to determine the best LMN variant in terms of stability *and* approximation quality for a given input-output data sequence. However, it is a versatile method to compare the different LMNs *and* Lyapunov stability criteria. The usual method to compare different Lyapunov approaches is to vary two system parameters (see e.g. [36, 38, 43]). Within this 2-dimensional parameter space a point-wise analysis of the provable stability region for different Lyapunov approaches is used. However, the proposed approach fits to the workflow of system identification because the system parameters of the local system matrices are determined by the identification process and thus fixed for stability analysis.

3.4.3   Lyapunov's Direct Method

The stability of LMNs can be proved by Lyapunov's direct method. This general approach is based on a state space formulation of the system and one has to find a suitable Lyapunov function $V(x)$.

Definition 3.4 *A Lyapunov function basically has to satisfy four properties to prove* asymptotic *stability of a system, [18]:*

   i) $V(x(k) = \mathbf{0}) = 0$
   ii) $V(x(k)) > 0\ for\ x(k) \neq \mathbf{0}$
   iii) $V(x(k))$ *approaches infinity as* $\|x(k)\| \to \infty$
   iv) $\Delta V(x(k)) = V(k+1) - V(k) < 0,\ \forall k \in \mathbb{N}^+.$

Lemma 3.1 *For* exponential *stability, the Lyapunov function must satisfy i)-iii) of* *defninition 3.4 and decrease strictly monotonically over time k with a decay rate* $\alpha,\ 0 < \alpha < 1$:

$$V(k+1) - \alpha^2 V(k) \leq 0,\ \forall k \in \mathbb{N}^+ \tag{3.9}$$

The proof of Lemma 3.1 is given in [45].

3.4.4 State-Space Notation for Open Loop Stability Analysis

For stability analysis and controller design using Lyapunov theory it is necessary to transform the LMN (2.14) into state-space notation. Several state space notations are possible. Depending whether open loop or closed loop/controller design is investigated different representations are suitable. Thus, in this section a minimal state-space model is introduced which uses an adapted controllability canonical form. The used model structure is depiced in Figure 3.6.

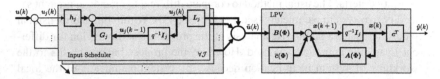

Figure 3.6 A LMN as minimal state space system

According to Figure 3.6 the LMN consists of two parts where the main advantage of this separation is, that the system matrix $A(\Phi)$ has minimal state-space configuration. The used Lyapunov based stability criteria of this work consider the local system matrices and thus bring advantages regarding the calculation effort.

- **Input Scheduler** generates time shifted input vectors
  The Input Scheduler generates for each input u_j a vector

$$
u_{\mathcal{J}}(k) = \begin{pmatrix} u_{\mathcal{J}}(k) \\ u_{\mathcal{J}}(k-1) \\ \vdots \\ u_{\mathcal{J}}(k - \max(\mathcal{M}_{\mathcal{J}}) + 1) \end{pmatrix}, \quad u_{\mathcal{J}}(k) \in \mathbb{R}^{M_{\mathcal{J}} \times 1} \tag{3.10}
$$

with contains past inputs. The following linear state space system generates the input vector:

$$
u_{\mathcal{J}}(k) = G_{\mathcal{J}} u_{\mathcal{J}}(k-1) + h_{\mathcal{J}} u_{\mathcal{J}}(k) \tag{3.11}
$$
$$
\tilde{u}_{\mathcal{J}}(k) = L_{\mathcal{J}} u_{\mathcal{J}}(k)
$$

with

$$G_{\mathcal{J}} = \begin{bmatrix} \mathbf{0}_{1 \times M_{\mathcal{J}}} \\ I_{M_{\mathcal{J}}-1} \; \mathbf{0}_{M_{\mathcal{J}}-1 \times 1} \end{bmatrix}, \quad h_{\mathcal{J}} = \begin{bmatrix} 1 \\ \mathbf{0}_{M_{\mathcal{J}}-1 \times 1} \end{bmatrix}, \quad L_{\mathcal{J}} = \begin{bmatrix} l^T_{\mathcal{J}.M_{\mathcal{J}}(1)} \\ \vdots \\ l^T_{\mathcal{J}.M_{\mathcal{J}}(|M_{\mathcal{J}}|)} \end{bmatrix},$$

$$G_{\mathcal{J}} \in \mathbb{R}^{M_{\mathcal{J}} \times M_{\mathcal{J}}}$$
$$h_{\mathcal{J}} \in \mathbb{R}^{M_{\mathcal{J}} \times 1}$$
$$L_{\mathcal{J}} \in \mathbb{R}^{|M_{\mathcal{J}}| \times M_{\mathcal{J}}}$$

$$l^T_{\mathcal{J}.M_{\mathcal{J}}}(1, m_{\mathcal{J}}) = \begin{cases} 1, & m_{\mathcal{J}} \in M_{\mathcal{J}} \\ 0, & \text{otherwise} \end{cases}, \quad \forall \{m_{\mathcal{J}} \in \mathbb{N} | 1 \le m_{\mathcal{J}} \le M_{\mathcal{J}}\}, \quad l^T_{\mathcal{J}.M_{\mathcal{J}}} \in \mathbb{R}^{1 \times M_{\mathcal{J}}}$$

The notation $I_{M_{\mathcal{J}}-1}$ stands for the identity matrix of dimension $M_{\mathcal{J}} - 1 \times M_{\mathcal{J}} - 1$ and $M_{\mathcal{J}}(i)$ stands for the i-th element of the set $M_{\mathcal{J}}$ and $l^T_{\mathcal{J}.M_{\mathcal{J}}}(1, i)$ stands for the i-th element of the vector $l^T_{\mathcal{J}.M_{\mathcal{J}}}$.
The vectors (3.10) are merged to a global input vector of the LVP System:

$$\hat{u}(k) = \begin{pmatrix} u_1(k) \\ \vdots \\ u_J(k) \end{pmatrix}, \quad u(k) \in \mathbb{R}^{(\sum_{\mathcal{J}} |M_{\mathcal{J}}|) \times 1} \tag{3.12}$$

Remark 3.2 *The input scheduler shifts the input through its states. Thus, the input scheduler is guaranteed stable because all eigenvalues are zero.*

- **LPV (Linear Parameter Varying System)** describes the eigendynamics of the LMN
  The transformation of the LMN (2.14) into the LPV system is very similar to the transformation of linear transfer functions into controllability canonical state space systems. The discrete state space notation of LMN can be defined as:

$$x(k+1) = A(\Phi)x(k) + B(\Phi)u(k) + f(\Phi) \tag{3.13}$$
$$\hat{y}(k) = c^T x(k)$$

with

$$A(\Phi) = \sum_{\mathcal{I}} \Phi_i(\tilde{x}(k))A_i, \; A_i \in \mathbb{R}^{N \times N} \tag{3.14}$$

$$B(\Phi) = \sum_{\mathcal{I}} \Phi_i(\tilde{x}(k))B_i, \; B_i \in \mathbb{R}^{N \times (\sum_{\mathcal{J}} |M_{\mathcal{J}}|)} \tag{3.15}$$

$$f(\mathbf{\Phi}) = \sum_{\mathcal{I}} \Phi_i(\tilde{\mathbf{x}}(k)) f_i, \quad f_i \in \mathbb{R}^{N \times 1} \tag{3.16}$$

where the validity functions of the local models are denoted as vector:

$$\mathbf{\Phi}^T(\tilde{\mathbf{x}}(k)) = [\Phi_1 \cdots \Phi_i \cdots \Phi_I], \quad \mathbf{\Phi}^T(\tilde{\mathbf{x}}(k)) \in \mathbb{R}^{1 \times I} \tag{3.17}$$

The state vector $\mathbf{x}(k)$ is defined as follows

$$\mathbf{x}(k) = \begin{pmatrix} \hat{y}(k - N + 1) \\ \vdots \\ \hat{y}(k) \end{pmatrix}, \quad \mathbf{x}(k) \in \mathbb{R}^{N \times 1} \tag{3.18}$$

The local system matrices A_i are denoted in controllability canonical form:

$$A_i = \begin{bmatrix} \mathbf{0}^{N-1 \times 1} & I_{N-1} \\ a_i^T \end{bmatrix}, \quad A_i \in \mathbb{R}^{N \times N}, \quad \forall \mathcal{I} \tag{3.19}$$

with

$$a_i^T(1, n) = \begin{cases} a_{N+1-n}^{(i)}, & n \in \mathcal{N} \\ 0, & \text{otherwise} \end{cases}, \quad \forall \{n \in \mathbb{N} | 1 \leq n \leq N\}, \quad a_i^T \in \mathbb{R}^{1 \times N}, \quad \forall \mathcal{I} \tag{3.20}$$

The local input matrices B_i are denoted as follows:

$$B_i = \begin{bmatrix} \mathbf{0}^{N-1 \times (\sum_{\mathcal{J}} |\mathcal{M}_{\mathcal{J}}|)} \\ b_i^T \end{bmatrix}, \quad B_i \in \mathbb{R}^{N \times (\sum_{\mathcal{J}} |\mathcal{M}_{\mathcal{J}}|)}, \quad \forall \mathcal{I} \tag{3.21}$$

with

$$b_i^T = \begin{bmatrix} b_{1.\mathcal{M}_1}^{(i)} \cdots b_{J.\mathcal{M}_J}^{(i)} \end{bmatrix}, \quad b_i^T \in \mathbb{R}^{1 \times (\sum_{\mathcal{J}} |\mathcal{M}_{\mathcal{J}}|)}, \quad \forall \mathcal{I}$$

The local bias terms f_i are as follows:

$$f_i = \begin{bmatrix} \mathbf{0}^{N-1 \times 1} \\ c^{(i)} \end{bmatrix}, \quad f_i \in \mathbb{R}^{N \times 1}$$

The (static) output vector $\mathbf{c}^T$ is denoted as:

$$\mathbf{c}^T = \begin{bmatrix} \mathbf{0}^{1 \times N-1} & 1 \end{bmatrix}, \quad \bar{\mathbf{c}}^T \in \mathbb{R}^{1 \times N} \tag{3.22}$$

Remark 3.3 *The LPV system depends on internal states and therefore the parameter variation is at least partially internally controlled. Thus, it is much more difficult to prove stability of such LPV systems compared to externally controlled one.*

3.4.5   Common Quadratic Lyapunov Approach for Discrete-Time Local Model Networks

The common quadratic Lyapunov approach was the first stability criterion to be proposed for LMNs, [18]. It aims to find one common quadratic Lyapunov function for all local models, see Figure 3.7:

$$V(k) = x^T(k)Px(k) > 0, \ \forall k \in \mathbb{N}^+ \tag{3.23}$$

Thus, the LMI solver has to find a single positive defninite matrix and must simultaneously satisfy as many LMIs as there are local models. This usually leads to conservatism due to the fact that by increasing the number of local models it will be more difficult to find a common Lyapunov function, [44, 50].

Figure 3.7 Common Quadratic Lyapunov Function

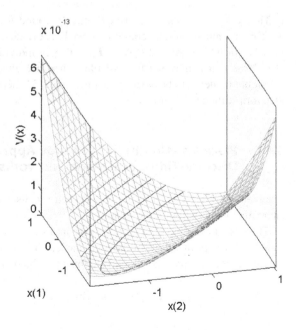

The common quadratic Lyapunov approach from [18, Theroem 4.2] is extended by the decay rate according to Lemma 3.1:

Theorem 3.1 *The dynamic LMN is globally exponentially stable with the decay rate α if there exists* a common positive definite matrix P *for all local models:*

$$P \succ 0 \tag{3.24}$$

such that the following conditions are satisfied:

$$\inf\{0 < \alpha < 1 : A_i^T P A_i \prec \alpha^2 P\}, \ \forall i \in \mathcal{I}. \tag{3.25}$$

The Proof of Theorem 3.1 follows from [18] and Lemma 3.1 and is given in Appendix B.1.

Remark 3.4 *The LMI solver* gevp *of MATLAB® Robust Control Toolbox^{TM} minimizes α and calculates P under the LMI constraints* (3.24) *and* (3.25) *of Theorem 3.1* simultaneously. *Thus, the resulting α can be seen as the infimum of the given problem.*

In Theorem 3.1 a *common* matrix P must be found for *all* local system matrices A_i. This is a much stronger condition than the individual stability of the local linear models, for which only $A_i^T P_i A_i - P_i \prec 0$ with individual P_i would be required, [10]. Note that it may not be possible to find a P that satisfies (3.25), although the global model may be asymptotically stable, [31, Section 4.2]. Theorem (3.1) is therefore sufficient but not necessary.

3.4.6 Piecewise Quadratic Lyapunov Approach for Discrete-Time Local Model Networks

The piecewise quadratic Lyapunov approach for discrete-time LMNs requires an alternative formulation of the system.

The basic idea is to split the state space into subspaces S_i which are defnined by using the validity functions of the local models. Thus, each local model defnines a corresponding subspace S_i which is defnined in the partition space as follows:

$$S_i = \{x | \Phi_i(\tilde{x}) \geq \Phi_j(\tilde{x}), \ j \in \mathcal{I}, j \neq i\} \ \forall i \in \mathcal{I}. \tag{3.26}$$

Note that the subspaces S_i depend on the structure of the validity functions, see Figure 2.2. Within these subspaces the local dynamics are characterized by the corresponding system matrix A_i of the local model with the additional disturbance term $\Delta A_i(\Phi)$ which describes the influence of interacting local models. Thus, (3.13) can also be expressed for each subspace S_i as

$$x(k+1) = (A_i + \Delta A_i(\Phi))x(k) + (B_i + \Delta B_i(\Phi))u(k) + (f_i + \Delta f_i(\Phi)), \; x(k) \in S_i$$
$$(3.27)$$

where

$$\Delta A_i(\Phi) = \sum_{j \in \mathcal{I} \setminus i} \Phi_j \Delta A_{ij}, \; \Delta A_i \in \mathbb{R}^{N \times N} \tag{3.28a}$$

$$\Delta B_i(\Phi) = \sum_{j \in \mathcal{I} \setminus i} \Phi_j \Delta B_{ij}, \; \Delta B_i \in \mathbb{R}^{N \times (\sum_{\mathcal{J}} |\mathcal{M}_{\mathcal{J}}|)} \tag{3.28b}$$

$$\Delta f_i(\Phi) = \sum_{j \in \mathcal{I} \setminus i} \Phi_j \Delta f_{ij}, \; \Delta f_i \in \mathbb{R}^{N \times 1} \tag{3.28c}$$

$$\Delta A_{ij} = A_j - A_i, \quad \Delta B_{ij} = B_j - B_i, \quad \Delta f_{ij} = f_j - f_i, \; i \in \mathcal{I}, \; j \in \mathcal{I} \setminus i.$$

The influences of interacting local models are summarized in $\Delta A_i(\Phi)$, $\Delta B_i(\Phi)$ and $\Delta f_i(\Phi)$, see (3.28a), (3.28b) and (3.28c).

The disturbance terms $\Delta A_i(\Phi)$ have a particular meaning for the piecewise quadratic Lyapunov approach because they constitute so-called uncertainty terms $\Delta A_i^T(\Phi)\Delta A_i(\Phi)$ in the LMI, [30]. For the purpose of stability analysis the following upper bounds $E_{iA}^T E_{iA}$ for the uncertainty terms of the subspaces (3.27) are introduced:

$$\Delta A_i(\Phi)^T \Delta A_i(\Phi) \preceq E_{iA}^T E_{iA}, \; \forall i \in \mathcal{I}. \tag{3.29}$$

where the particular validity function vector Φ for which the equality sign of (3.29) holds is a priori unknown.

Remark 3.5 *The upper bounds of the uncertainty terms lead to conservatism of the resulting stability analysis [29, 31], especially for the worst case bounds presented in [51, 52]. Thus in [51, 52] and Section 3.4.8 advanced methods are presented which approximate the upper bounds and lead to less conservatism. For systems with local dynamics in controllability canonical form an optimization based method is introduced in Section 3.4.8 and [50], respectively. For switching systems with hard-limit validity functions, [32], and/or continuous time systems [33], the upper bounds of the uncertainty terms do not appear and the piecewise quadratic Lyapunov* *approach is less conservative than for discrete-time LMNs with overlapping validity functions.*

To prove global stability, *local* quadratic Lyapunov functions have to be found for all subspaces, see Figure 3.8, which are linked by feasible transitions from one subspace into another. Consequently, the Lyapunov functions must decrease at each timestep, even if the state transits from one subspace into another to satisfy (3.9), [30].

Figure 3.8 Piecewise Quadratic Lyapunov Function

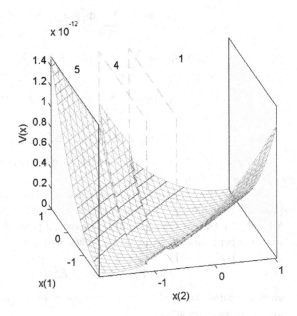

Theorem 3.2 follows by extending [30, Theorem 3.1] with the decay rate according to Lemma 3.1:

Theorem 3.2 *The dynamic LMN is exponentially stable in the region*

$$S = \bigcup_{i \in \mathcal{I}} S_i, \tag{3.30}$$

which is the union of the subspaces S_i, if there exists a set of symmetric positive definite matrices P_i:

$$P_i \succ 0, \ \forall i \in \mathcal{I} \tag{3.31}$$

such that the following conditions are satisfied:

$$\inf \left\{ 0 < \alpha < 1 : \begin{bmatrix} A_i^T P_j A_i + \frac{1}{\varepsilon} E_{iA}^T E_{iA} & A_i^T P_j \\ P_j A_i & P_j - \frac{1}{\varepsilon} I \end{bmatrix} \prec \alpha^2 \begin{bmatrix} P_i & 0 \\ 0 & 0 \end{bmatrix} \right\},$$
$$\varepsilon > 0, \ \forall i \in \mathcal{I}, \ j \in \Omega_i^p \tag{3.32}$$

where the set Ω_i^p denotes those local models where a transition from model i is possible, that is

$$\Omega_i^p = \left\{ j | (\tilde{x}(k) \in S_i \wedge \tilde{x}(k+1) \in S_j), \ j \in \mathcal{I} \right\}, \ \forall i \in \mathcal{I}. \tag{3.33}$$

This includes the case $i = j$ which requires that every local model must have stable dynamics as a necessary condition. The case $i \neq j$ requires that the piece-wise Lyapunov function decreases when the system state transits across the region boundary from S_i to S_j. To prove global stability S has to cover the whole partition space.

The proof of Theorem 3.2 follows from [30] and Lemma 3.1 and is given in Appendix B.2.

Remark 3.6 *Ω_i^p is crucial in reducing dimensionality of the LMI problem.*

Remark 3.7 *The* gevp *solver provided by MATLAB® Robust Control Toolbox™ requires a positive defininite matrix on the right hand side of (3.32). Thus (3.32) is reformulated to:*

$$\inf \left\{ 0 < \alpha < 1 : Z_i \preceq \alpha^2 P_i \right\} \forall i \in \mathcal{I} \tag{3.34}$$

such that

$$\begin{bmatrix} A_i^T P_j A_i + \frac{1}{\varepsilon} E_{iA}^T E_{iA} & A_i^T P_j \\ P_j A_i & P_j - \frac{1}{\varepsilon} I \end{bmatrix} \prec \begin{bmatrix} Z_i & 0 \\ 0 & 0 \end{bmatrix}, \ \varepsilon > 0, \ \forall i \in \mathcal{I}, \ j \in \Omega_i^p \tag{3.35}$$

Remark 3.8 *Since the P_i and the $E_{iA}^T E_{iA}$ matrices are symmetric the right hand side of (3.34) is also symmetric.*

Since the dynamics of the local models are denoted in controllability canonical form the uncertainty terms can be expressed as:

$$\Delta A_i(\boldsymbol{\Phi}) = \begin{bmatrix} \mathbf{0}_{n-1 \times n} \\ \Delta \bar{a}_i^T(\boldsymbol{\Phi}) \end{bmatrix}, \ \Delta \bar{a}_i^T(\boldsymbol{\Phi}) \in \mathbb{R}^{1 \times N} \tag{3.36}$$

where $\Delta \bar{a}_i^T(\boldsymbol{\Phi})$ denotes the weighted aggregation of the last row of ΔA_i according to (3.36):

$$\Delta \bar{a}_i^T(\boldsymbol{\Phi}) = \tilde{\boldsymbol{\Phi}}_i^T \tilde{A}_i \tag{3.37}$$

with

$$\tilde{A}_i = \begin{bmatrix} \Delta \bar{a}_{i1} \ \ldots \ \Delta \bar{a}_{ij} \ \ldots \ \Delta \bar{a}_{iI} \end{bmatrix}^T, \ \tilde{A}_i \in \mathbb{R}^{I-1 \times N}$$

$$\tilde{\boldsymbol{\Phi}}_i(\tilde{x}(k)) = \begin{bmatrix} \tilde{\Phi}_{i1} \ \ldots \ \tilde{\Phi}_{ij} \ \ldots \ \tilde{\Phi}_{iI} \end{bmatrix}^T, \ \tilde{\boldsymbol{\Phi}}_i \in \mathbb{R}^{I-1 \times 1}$$

$$\Delta \bar{a}_{ij}^T = \bar{a}_j^T - \bar{a}_i^T, \ \bar{a}_i^T = \begin{bmatrix} 0 \ \ldots \ 0 \ 1 \end{bmatrix} A_i$$

$$\Delta \bar{a}_{ij}^T \in \mathbb{R}^{1 \times N}, \ \tilde{x}(k) \in S_i, \ \forall i, j \in \mathcal{I}, \ j \neq i.$$

$\tilde{\Phi}_{ij}$ denotes the validity function of model j in subspace S_i. The validity function of all models is bounded in each subspace S_i. The validity function of the nominal model i, which does not appear in $\tilde{\boldsymbol{\Phi}}_i$, has a lower limit $\tilde{\Phi}_{ii,min}$ in S_i. All other models ($j \in \mathcal{I}, \ j \neq i$) have an upper bound $\tilde{\Phi}_{ij,max}$ in S_i. All these bounds are defnined by values of the respective validity functions at the hull of the subspace S_i and have to be determined by a proper method which depends on the architecture of the considered LMN. For LMNs with an hierarchical discriminant tree [9] a proper method is proposed in Section 3.4.7.

3.4.7   Determination of the Convex Hull of Local Model Networks with a Hierarchical Discriminant Tree

Due to the fact that the dimension of LMNs partition spaces is arbitrary the presented method is dimension independent. The local models of LMN with a hierarchical discriminant tree are defined by hyperplanes where their most important properties are:

- A hyperplane in an n-dimensional space has a dimension of $n - 1$
- To determine a point in an n-dimensional hyperspace n-hyperplanes of dimension $n - 1$ have to be intersected to get the unique solution

---

Algorithm 1: Convex Hull of the local models

---

begin

   Generate the hyperplanes of the partition space boundaries

   Calculate the corner points of the partition space boundaries

   Generate the intersection point of the i-th hyperplane, see Figure 2.4:

   for $i \in$ *model tree nodes* **do**

      Intersect hyperplane i with a permuted set of $n - 1$ hyperplanes

      Test validity of all points (see Figure 3.9)

      Split valid points for the lower nodes:

      for *valid points* **do**

         New points to both lower nodes

         Old points are split according to their new validity between the

         lower nodes

3.4.8   Determination of the Upper Bounds of the Uncertainty Terms

Existing methods only approximate the upper bounds and the determination is also very conservative because it uses the maximum eigenvalue of the uncertainty terms without considering the validity function, [53]:

$$\overline{\lambda}_i = \max(\lambda_{max}(\Delta A_{ij}^T \Delta A_{ij})) \tag{3.38}$$

$$E_{iA}^T E_{iA} = \overline{\lambda}_i I, \; I \in \mathbb{R}^{n \times n}, \tag{3.39}$$

Furthermore, existing methods are only applicable to simple partitioning strategies or low dimensional partition spaces, respectively. Thus, an accurate determination of the upper bounds of the uncertainty terms is described in this section.

    Since the piecewise quadratic Lyapunov approach should be as little conservative as possible the upper bounds $E_{iA}^T E_{iA}$ should be as small as possible. To prove stability using the piecewise Lyapunov approach the upper bounds have to be chosen according to the *worst occurring* uncertainty $\Delta A_i(\Phi)^T \Delta A_i(\Phi)$. Otherwise the criterion can become unnecessarily conservative as presented and described in [51], [52] and [53]. Thus, the upper bounds of the uncertainty terms should be *as small as possible* and have to be determined as conservative as *necessary*. For LMNs with system dynamics denoted in controllability canonical form according to

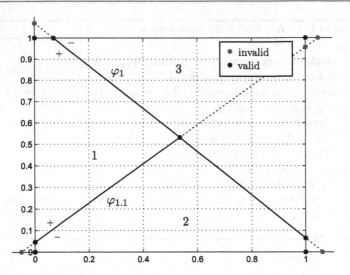

Figure 3.9 Exemplary hyperplane intersection

(2.14) the upper bounds can be accurately determined by the constrained quadratic optimization. The method is stated in the following theorem:

Theorem 3.3 *The upper bounds of the uncertainty terms of the LMN (3.27), with system dynamics denoted in controllability canonical form,*

$$E_{iA}^T E_{iA} = \Delta A_i^T(\tilde{\Phi}_i) \Delta A_i(\tilde{\Phi}_i), \ \forall i \in \mathcal{I} \tag{3.40}$$

are defined by the most conservative feasible validity function vectors $\tilde{\Phi}_i$ which are determined from the constrained optimization

$$J_i = arg \max_{\tilde{\Phi}_i} \tilde{\Phi}_i^T (\tilde{A}_i \tilde{A}_i^T) \tilde{\Phi}_i$$

$$subject \ to \ \begin{cases} \sum_{j=\mathcal{I}, j\neq i} \tilde{\Phi}_{ij} = 1 - \tilde{\Phi}_{ii,min} \\ 0 \leq \tilde{\Phi}_{ij} \leq \tilde{\Phi}_{ij,max} \end{cases}$$

$$\forall i, j \in \mathcal{I}, \ j \neq i \tag{3.41}$$

The proof of Theorem 3.3 is given in appendix B.3.

3.4.9   Example

For illustrative purposes a stable second order Wiener model is considered. It consists of a dynamic linear block with a normalized transfer function $G_L(z) = V(z)/U(z)$ in cascade with a static nonlinearity $f(v)$ at the output with v as the intermediate variable at the output of the linear block, see 3.10 [54].

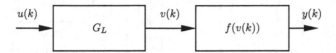

Figure 3.10 Wiener Model

For the present simulation results $G_L(z)$ and $f(v)$ were chosen as

$$G_L(z) = \frac{0.3007z^{-1} + 0.2812z^{-2}}{1 - 0.8426z^{-1} + 0.6478z^{-2}} \tag{3.42}$$

$$y(k) = f(v(k)) = \arctan(v(k)). \tag{3.43}$$

Despite their simple structure Wiener systems enable a simple representation of nonlinear systems. The nonlinearity $f(v)$ has full impact on the output and stability analysis can become challenging, in particular when the nonlinearity has a saturation character like in the present example, [1, 55].

In this example the input $u(k)$ is bounded by the interval $[-3, \ 3]$.

Figure 3.11 demonstrates the oscillatory behavior of both the original system and the LMN. For system identification an excitation signal was generated to capture the nonlinear process, [56].

From these data an LMN comprising eight local models and second order dynamics was generated by the algorithm presented in [9], where the partition space is defined by the model input and output

$$\tilde{x}(k) = [u(k-1) \ \hat{y}(k-1)]. \tag{3.44}$$

The generated validity functions and the identification data sequence are illustrated in Figure 3.12.

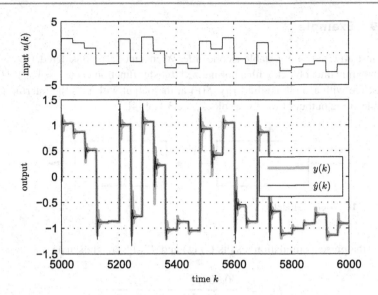

Figure 3.11 In- and output of the system and the LMN

Figure 3.12 Wiener
Model: Partition space and
identification data sequence

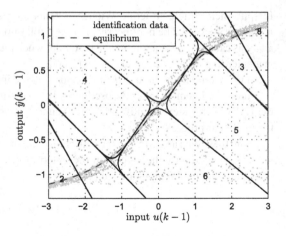

The following system matrices are obtained from the LMN when the discrete transfer functions of the local linear dynamics are represented in controllability canonical form:

$$A_1 = \begin{bmatrix} 0 & 1 \\ -0.596 & 0.68 \end{bmatrix}, \quad A_2 = \begin{bmatrix} 0 & 1 \\ -0.237 & 0.546 \end{bmatrix}$$

$$A_3 = \begin{bmatrix} 0 & 1 \\ -0.312 & 0.604 \end{bmatrix}, \quad A_4 = \begin{bmatrix} 0 & 1 \\ -0.559 & 0.871 \end{bmatrix}$$

$$A_5 = \begin{bmatrix} 0 & 1 \\ -0.544 & 0.867 \end{bmatrix}, \quad A_6 = \begin{bmatrix} 0 & 1 \\ -0.602 & 0.672 \end{bmatrix} \tag{3.45}$$

$$A_7 = \begin{bmatrix} 0 & 1 \\ -0.307 & 0.606 \end{bmatrix}, \quad A_8 = \begin{bmatrix} 0 & 1 \\ -0.235 & 0.55 \end{bmatrix}$$

The subspaces S_i are illustrated in Figure 3.13.

The local models have strongly differing eigenvalues which is illustrated in Figure 3.14.

The upper bounds of the uncertainty terms of the local models directly follow from the following uncertainty vectors $\Delta \bar{a}_i^T (\tilde{\Phi}_i)$ which are determined using Theorem 3.3, (3.40) and (B.3).

Figure 3.13 Wiener Model: Subspaces

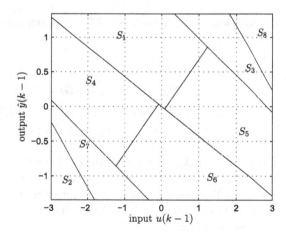

Figure 3.14 Wiener
Model: Eigenvalues of the
local models

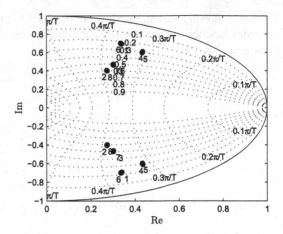

$$\Delta \bar{a}_1^T(\tilde{\Phi}_1) = \begin{bmatrix} 0.155 & 0.009 \end{bmatrix} \quad \Delta \bar{a}_2^T(\tilde{\Phi}_2) = \begin{bmatrix} -0.044 & 0.04 \end{bmatrix}$$

$$\Delta \bar{a}_3^T(\tilde{\Phi}_3) = \begin{bmatrix} -0.129 & 0.135 \end{bmatrix} \quad \Delta \bar{a}_4^T(\tilde{\Phi}_4) = \begin{bmatrix} 0.132 & -0.188 \end{bmatrix}$$

$$\Delta \bar{a}_5^T(\tilde{\Phi}_5) = \begin{bmatrix} 0.118 & -0.185 \end{bmatrix} \quad \Delta \bar{a}_6^T(\tilde{\Phi}_6) = \begin{bmatrix} 0.162 & 0.0152 \end{bmatrix} \qquad (3.46)$$

$$\Delta \bar{a}_7^T(\tilde{\Phi}_7) = \begin{bmatrix} -0.14 & 0.136 \end{bmatrix} \quad \Delta \bar{a}_8^T(\tilde{\Phi}_8) = \begin{bmatrix} -0.047 & 0.0367 \end{bmatrix}$$

The following model transitions (3.47) are determined using the algorithm presented in Section 3.5:

$$\Omega_1 = \{1, \ 3, \ 4, \ 5, \ 6\}, \ \ \Omega_2 = \{2, \ 7\},$$
$$\Omega_3 = \{1, \ 3, \ 5, \ 8\}, \ \ \Omega_4 = \{1, \ 4, \ 6, \ 7\},$$
$$\Omega_5 = \{1, \ 3, \ 5, \ 6\}, \ \ \Omega_6 = \{1, \ 4, \ 5, \ 6, \ 7\}, \qquad (3.47)$$
$$\Omega_7 = \{2, \ 4, \ 6, \ 7\}, \ \ \Omega_8 = \{3, \ 8\}$$

Using (3.40), (B.3), (3.45), (3.46) and (3.47) for the piecewise quadratic Lyapunov approach, according to Theorem 3.2, set $\alpha = 1$ for simplicity and using the MAT-LAB LMI Toolbox® positive definite P_i matrices can be determined which satisfy (3.31) and (3.32). Thus it is guaranteed, that the considered LMN is exponentially stable in the region $\mathcal{S}$.

In contrast using the more conservative approximation of the upper bounds (3.38) it is not possible to find a solution to the LMIs and thus to prove stability of the LMN.

Table 3.1 shows the significant reduction of the maximum eigenvalue of the upper bounds compared to the more conservative approximation.

Table 3.1 Wiener Model: Maximum eigenvalue of the upper bounds

Model #	Method		Reduction
	(3.38)	(3.41)	
	classical	new	
1	0.1475	0.024	83.7%
2	0.2092	0.0035	98.3%
3	0.1318	0.0347	73.7%
4	0.2092	0.0528	74.8%
5	0.1974	0.0483	75.5%
6	0.15	0.0265	82.4%
7	0.1336	0.0378	71.7%
8	0.2084	0.0036	98.3%

For this example an average reduction of 82.3% is achieved. According to Lemma A.5 this is a significant reduction of the conservatism of the piecewise quadratic Lyapunov approach for LMNs with system dynamics in controllability canonical form.

For the considered LMN utilizing the proposed concept for the piecewise quadratic Lyapunov approach it is possible to prove stability. Using the classical method presented in [51], [52] and [53], which approximates the upper bounds, no solution for the LMIs can be found and consequently the criterion fails to prove stability although the considered LMN is stable.

3.4.10 Fuzzy Lyapunov Approach for Discrete-Time Local Model Networks

The fuzzy Lyapunov approach [29, 34, 35, 57, 58] aims to find a non-quadratic Lyapunov function for the global model, see Figure 3.15,

$$V(k) = x^T(k) \left(\sum_{\mathcal{I}} \Phi_i(\tilde{x}(k)) P_i \right) x(k) > 0, \ \forall k \in \mathbb{N}^+, \tag{3.48}$$

with individual positive defninite P_i matrices. Note that each local model indepen-
dently satisfies (3.23) (there is an individual P_i matrix associated with each local
model).

Figure 3.15 Fuzzy
Lyapunov Function

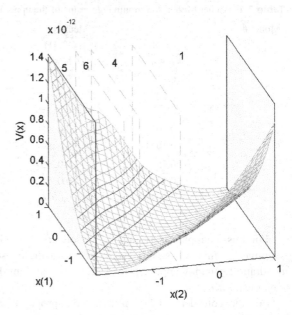

Remark 3.9 *The validity functions* Φ_i *in (3.48) are equivalent to those of the local
models in (2.14).*

For asymptotic stability all local models must be stable as a prerequisite. Furthermore, every possible trajectory must satisfy iv) of defninition (3.4). This shows, that
the feasible model transitions are of high interest when using the fuzzy Lyapunov
approach. Theorem 3.4 follows by extending the Main Theorem of [34] with the
decay rate according to Lemma 3.1:

Theorem 3.4 *An LMN is exponentially stable with the decay rate* α *in the region
U if there exists a set of positive definite matrices* P_i:

$$P_i \succ 0, \quad \forall i \in \mathcal{I} \tag{3.49}$$

such that the following conditions are satisfied:

$$\inf \left\{ 0 < \alpha < 1 : A_i^T P_j A_i \prec \alpha^2 P_i \right\}, \; \forall i \in \mathcal{I}, j \in \Omega_i^f \qquad (3.50)$$

where the set Ω_i^f defines all possible model transitions of model i within region U, [34]. By using the dominant region of a local model, according to (3.26) the possible transitions can be defined, as

$$\Omega_i^f = \left\{ j | (\tilde{x}(k) \in S_i \wedge \tilde{x}(k+1) \in S_j) \vee (\tilde{x}(k) \in S_j \wedge \tilde{x}(k+1) \in S_i), \; j \in \mathcal{I} \right\}, \; \forall i \in \mathcal{I} \qquad (3.51)$$

and contain the model indices where a transition is possible from model i to j and from j to i within region U. This includes the case $i = j$ which requires that every local model must have stable dynamics as a necessary condition.

The proof of Theorem 3.4 follows from [34] and Lemma 3.1 and is given in Appendix B.4.

Remark 3.10 *In recent years, the fuzzy Lyapunov approach was refined in several works, see [38, 39, 40, 41, 42, 59, 60]. These approaches have shown, that they are less conservative than previous approaches. However, this work aims to give an overview and the presented extension with the decay rate can also be applied to these approaches.*

3.5   Transition Determination

3.5.1   General

From the stability criteria discussed so far it is evident that the number of LMIs to be satisfied is critical for the success to prove stability. The more interactions between local models exist, the more LMIs have to be satisfied which in turn reduces the chance to successfully prove stability. Each transition requires *one additional LMI* for the piecewise quadratic Lyapunov approach, see (3.33), and *two additional LMIs* for the fuzzy Lyapunov approach, see (3.51). Thus, the difficulty of finding a suitable Lyapunov function is increased when additional model transitions are taken into account. Therefore, a proper determination of the feasible model transitions will help to reduce conservatism or even makes a stability proof of complex LMNs possible at all. Thus, in this section a method for the determination of all feasible model transitions is proposed. For such a methodology its applicability to as many partitioning strategies as possible, see Figure 2.2, and the type of validity function, see Figure 2.3, is important.

If no information about the model transitions is available, then transitions between all models must be taken into account:

$$\Omega_i^q = \Omega_i^f = \mathcal{I}, \quad \forall i \in \mathcal{I}. \tag{3.52}$$

The proposed methodology determines the possible transitions in an LMN by utilizing an optimally designed excitation data sequence. As a consequence the stability region U is aimed to be identical to the convex hull of the used data sequence. In contrast, most available stability criteria for LMNs aim to show *unbounded* global stability (e.g. [29, 31]) which can become too expensive when only a certain part of the LMN describes the actual dynamic operating range of the process. Nevertheless, it cannot be ruled out that outside of this hull unnoticed transitions occur. However, for the design of controllers or observers, stability close to or beyond that boundary is of only limited interest.

It must be noted, nevertheless, that the characteristics of the excitation data significantly contribute to the effectiveness of the proposed method. This is not a severe disadvantage, because in data-driven models the range of the identification data is a priori defnined as the area of interest (e.g. operating area) and usually problem specific design of experiments (DoE, [56]) is employed.

3.5.2 Methodology

The information about the model transitions of the LMN will be represented by a so-called *transition matrix* Ξ. It is based on the excitation data sequence and the method to generate it will be described in the following.

The excitation signals $\boldsymbol{u}_{\mathcal{J}}(k)$, which are generated by a proper DoE [56] and the model output $\hat{\boldsymbol{y}}(k)$, which is generated by simulating the process using the considered LMN with the excitation signal, are merged to a matrix

$$\boldsymbol{L}(k) = [\boldsymbol{u}_{\mathcal{J}}(k - \mathcal{M}) \, \hat{\boldsymbol{y}}(k - \mathcal{N})], \quad \forall k \in \mathcal{K}, \ \boldsymbol{L} \in \mathbb{R}^{K \times O} \tag{3.53}$$

the rows of which correspond to the regressor vector $\boldsymbol{r}(k)$. The ordered set of the samples of the data sequence is given by

$$\mathcal{K} = (k \in \mathbb{N} | 1 \leq k \leq K) \tag{3.54}$$

where K is the number of samples. Those signals which are used as input arguments
to the validity function form a subset of the data sequence. The choice of such a
particular subset is strongly dependent on the system's nonlinearities and is thus
usually done by the user. The input arguments to the validity function are denoted
by $\tilde{L}$ indicating that it is a sub-matrix of L

$$\tilde{L} = L(\mathcal{K}, \tilde{\mathcal{O}}), \ \tilde{L} \in \mathbb{R}^{K \times \tilde{O}} \tag{3.55}$$

the rows of which correspond to $\tilde{x}(k)$. Consequently, the output of a validity function
C can be formulated as

$$C(\mathcal{K}, \mathcal{I}) = \Phi_{\mathcal{I}}(\tilde{L}(\mathcal{K})), \ C \in \mathbb{R}^{K \times I}. \tag{3.56}$$

When the state trajectory evolves over time and transits through different local
models a matrix of indices of the two most dominant local models D (= local
models with maximum Φ) can be generated in a similar way as L by using C:

$$D(k) = \left[\{i_1 | C(k, i_1) = \max(C(k, \mathcal{I}))\} \{i_2 | C(k, i_2) = \max(C(k, \mathcal{I} \setminus i_1))\} \right], \ \forall k \in \mathcal{K},$$
$$D \in \mathbb{N}^{K \times 2}. \tag{3.57}$$

The matrices C and D inherently contain the relevant information required to determine the actual model transitions. They are used to generate the *transition matrix*
Ξ which compactly describes possible local model transits. Ξ is a square matrix
with boolean entries and has the following properties:

$$\dim \Xi = I \times I \tag{3.58}$$
$$\Xi(r, c) \in \{0, 1\}, \ \forall r, c \in \mathcal{I} \tag{3.59}$$

The elements of Ξ can be interpreted as follows:

$$\Xi(r, c) = 1 \text{ if there is a transition from model } r \text{ to } c$$
$$\text{and zero otherwise}$$

To generate the transition matrix Ξ two steps are necessary:

①   *Initialize Ξ as identity matrix*

$$\Xi = I_l \tag{3.60}$$

The main diagonal entries which formally refer to an interaction of a local model with itself must be set to one since the piecewise quadratic and the fuzzy Lyapunov approach require stable local models, [29].

②   *Set the feasible model transitions*

From (3.57) the two most dominant local models are determined for each sample. A valid transition is detected whenever the dominant models change or when the validity functions do not change by means of boolean algebra:

$$\boldsymbol{D}(k, 1) = \boldsymbol{D}(k - 1, 2) \wedge \boldsymbol{D}(k, 2) = \boldsymbol{D}(k - 1, 1) \vee \boldsymbol{C}(k, \mathcal{I}) = \boldsymbol{C}(k - 1, \mathcal{I}) \wedge \boldsymbol{D}(k, \mathcal{I}) \tag{3.61}$$

$$= \boldsymbol{D}(k - 1, \mathcal{I}), \ \forall k \in \mathcal{K} \tag{3.62}$$

Condition (3.62) is examined for all rows of $\boldsymbol{C}$ and $\boldsymbol{D}$, respectively. The detected transition directly follows when (3.62) is true for some k and the respective entry is set in the transition matrix:

$$\Xi(\boldsymbol{D}(k - 1, 1), \boldsymbol{D}(k, 1)) = 1 \tag{3.63}$$

The sets Ω_i^p, Ω_i^f which define the model transitions for the piecewise quadratic Lyapunov (3.33) and the fuzzy Lyapunov approach (3.51), respectively, directly follow from Ξ:

$$\Omega_i^p = \{j \,|\, \Xi(i, j) = 1, \ \forall j \in \mathcal{I}\}, \ \forall i \in \mathcal{I} \tag{3.64}$$

$$\Omega_i^f = \{j \,|\, \Xi(i, j) = 1 \vee \Xi(j, i) = 1, \ \forall j \in \mathcal{I}\}, \ \forall i \in \mathcal{I} \tag{3.65}$$

3.5.3   Examples

In Section 3.5.3.1 a simple example shows a single transition from one model to another. The effectiveness of the fuzzy Lyapunov approach in conjunction with the proposed method is demonstrated by means of an illustrative nonlinear process in Section 3.5.3.2.

3.5.3.1 Example: Single Transition

Figure 3.16(a) illustrates an exemplary trajectory of an identification data sequence with constant input $u(k)$ and the 50% contour lines of the validity functions of the local models. The timestep from $k = 2$ to $k = 3$ is considered in detail. The analysis of the trajectory by the proposed method for the transition determination is illustrated in Figure 3.16(b).

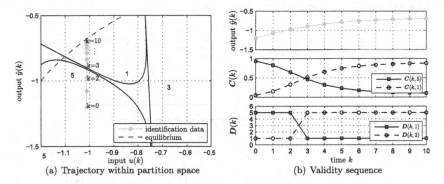

(a) Trajectory within partition space   (b) Validity sequence

Figure 3.16 Exemplary Transition from one local model to another

The upper plot of Figure 3.16(b) shows the system output over time, the middle one shows the validity function outputs of local models 1 and 5, and the bottom one illustrates how the two most dominant models were determined by (3.63).

At $k = 2$ local model 5 is most dominant ($D(2, 1) = 5$) and at $k = 3$ ($D(3, 1) = 1$) which indicates that model 1 is now dominating:

$$D(2, 1) = 5, \; D(2, 2) = 1, \; D(3, 1) = 1, \; D(3, 2) = 5 \tag{3.66}$$

Thus, according to (3.62) a valid transition is detected and the corresponding entry is set in the transition matrix according to (3.63):

$$\Xi\,(5, 1) = 1$$

3.5.3.2 Example: Transition Determination
For illustrative purposes a nonlinear dynamic process is considered, which possesses strongly operating point dependent dynamics. This process is adopted from [10], [61] and can be described by the following difference equation:

$$y(k) = 0.133u(k - 1) - 0.0677u(k - 2) + 1.5y(k - 1) \tag{3.67}$$
$$- 0.7y(k - 2) + u(k)[0.1y(k - 1) - 0.2y(k - 2)] \tag{3.68}$$

In this example the input $u(k)$ is bounded to the interval $[-1.5\ 0.5]$.

Figure 3.17 demonstrates that the system has weakly damped oscillatory behavior for large inputs whereas for small inputs strongly damped aperiodic behavior is present. For system identification an excitation signal was generated to capture both the nonlinear dynamic and static behavior, [56].

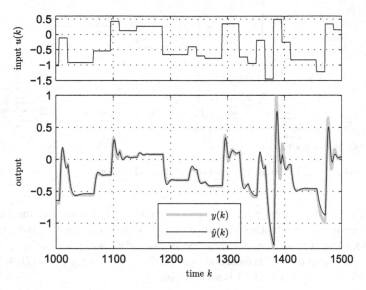

Figure 3.17 In- and output of the system and the LMN

From these data an LMN comprising six local models was generated by the algorithm presented in [22], where the local models are defined by an axis oblique decomposition of the partition space. Figure 3.18 shows the partition space

$$\tilde{x}(k) = [u(k-1)\ \hat{y}(k-1)] \tag{3.69}$$

as well as the identification data. The partitioning strategy of [22] uses statistical methods to avoid overfitting by local models generated with only few points.

The comparison of the system output and the output of the LMN in Figure 3.17 shows that the LMN is accurately approximating the system within the whole operating range.

The following system matrices are obtained from the LMN when the discrete-time transfer functions of the local linear dynamics are represented in controllability canonical form:

$$A_1 = \begin{bmatrix} 0 & 1 \\ -0.71 & 1.668 \end{bmatrix}, A_2 = \begin{bmatrix} 0 & 1 \\ -0.736 & 1.525 \end{bmatrix}$$

$$A_3 = \begin{bmatrix} 0 & 1 \\ -0.622 & 1.488 \end{bmatrix}, A_4 = \begin{bmatrix} 0 & 1 \\ -0.844 & 1.832 \end{bmatrix} \quad (3.70)$$

$$A_5 = \begin{bmatrix} 0 & 1 \\ -0.767 & 1.74 \end{bmatrix}, A_6 = \begin{bmatrix} 0 & 1 \\ -0.733 & 1.702 \end{bmatrix}$$

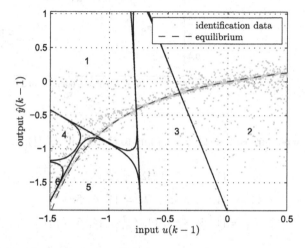

Figure 3.18 Partition space and identification data sequence

The local models have very different damping ratios, Figure 3.19 shows their eigenvalues for illustration.

3.5.3.3 Fuzzy Lyapunov Approach with Transition Determination
The following transition matrix is generated using the proposed method of Section 3.5:

$$\Xi = \begin{bmatrix} 1 & 0 & 1 & 1 & 1 & 0 \\ 0 & 1 & 1 & 0 & 0 & 0 \\ 1 & 1 & 1 & 0 & 1 & 0 \\ 1 & 0 & 0 & 1 & 1 & 1 \\ 1 & 0 & 1 & 1 & 1 & 1 \\ 0 & 0 & 0 & 1 & 1 & 1 \end{bmatrix} \quad (3.71)$$

Figure 3.19 Eigenvalues
of the local models

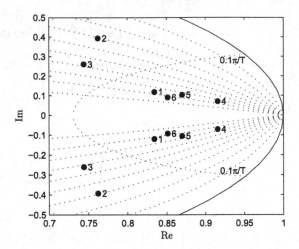

Defining the model transitions Ω_i^f, according to (3.51) with (3.71):

$$\Omega_1^f = \{1, \ 3, \ 4, \ 5\}, \quad \Omega_2^f = \{2, \ 3\},$$
$$\Omega_3^f = \{1, \ 2, \ 3, \ 5\}, \quad \Omega_4^f = \{1, \ 4, \ 5, \ 6\}, \qquad (3.72)$$
$$\Omega_5^f = \{1, \ 3, \ 4, \ 5, \ 6\}, \quad \Omega_6^f = \{4, \ 5, \ 6\}$$

for the fuzzy Lyapunov approach, according to Theorem 3.4 and using the MATLAB
LMI Toolbox® the following positive definite P_i matrices are determined:

$$P_1 = \begin{bmatrix} 0.14 & -0.152 \\ -0.152 & 0.175 \end{bmatrix}, \ P_2 = \begin{bmatrix} 0.715 & -0.726 \\ -0.726 & 0.856 \end{bmatrix}$$

$$P_3 = \begin{bmatrix} 0.082 & -0.086 \\ -0.086 & 0.1 \end{bmatrix}, \ P_4 = \begin{bmatrix} 0.191 & -0.209 \\ -0.209 & 0.237 \end{bmatrix}$$

$$P_5 = \begin{bmatrix} 0.148 & -0.162 \\ -0.162 & 0.188 \end{bmatrix}, \ P_6 = \begin{bmatrix} 0.139 & -0.153 \\ -0.153 & 0.177 \end{bmatrix}$$

which satisfy (3.49) and (3.50). Thus it is guaranteed, that the considered LMN is
asymptotically stable within U.

3.5.3.4 Common Quadratic- and Fuzzy Lyapunov Approach without Transition Determination

In this section it is assumed that no information about the model transitions is available for the fuzzy Lyapunov approach. Consequently all entries of Ξ are set to one. This leads to a more conservative result, because of additional LMIs. Thus, the classic fuzzy Lyapunov approach fails to prove stability of the considered LMN with six local models.

Using the common quadratic Lyapunov approach

$$A_i^T P A_i - P \prec 0 \tag{3.73}$$

for all A_i of (3.70) it is not possible to prove stability of the nonlinear dynamic process because of the different dynamic behavior. This is independent of the number of local models.

3.5.3.5 Influence of the Number of Local Models

For the considered LMN with six local models it is only possible to prove stability using the proposed concept. Using either the common quadratic Lyapunov approach or the Fuzzy Lyapunov approach without the proposed concept increasing the number of local models results in an increased complexity of the stability criterion because of additional LMIs. Thus, in this section the influence of the number of local models and the number of the considered transitions on the stability criteria will be shown. For that purpose four different LMNs, comprising three to six local models, are compared in the following. These LMNs are generated utilizing the same identification data sequence. Figure 3.20 illustrates that the complexity of the LMN is generally increased by the number of local models.

Figure 3.21 shows that the complexity of the fuzzy Lyapunov approach can be significantly reduced by using the proposed method, particularly for LMNs with a high number of local models.

Table 3.2 shows an overview of the common quadratic Lyapunov approach, the Fuzzy Lyapunov approach with all transitions as well as the Fuzzy Lyapunov approach using the proposed method. Further, the influence of the number of local models on the stability criteria is presented utilizing the considered nonlinear dynamic process.

The analysis of Table 3.2 shows that the conservatism of the Lyapunov approach can be generally reduced by using the proposed method because the number of LMIs is reduced in all cases. Further, it is even possible, that the conservatism decreases when the number of local models is increased. Using the common quadratic Lyapunov approach no stability proof is possible.

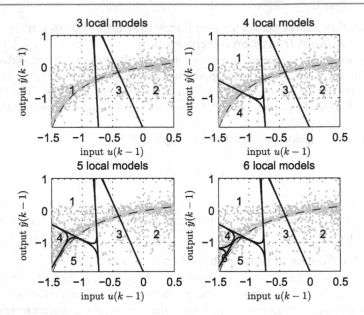

Figure 3.20 Partition Space of LMNs with different number of local models

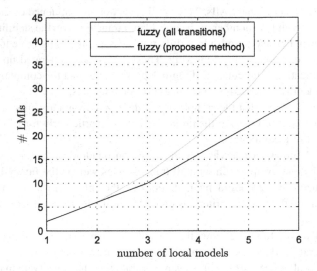

Figure 3.21 Number of LMIs of different stability criteria and different numbers of local models

Table 3.2 Nonlinear Dynamic Process: Stability criteria

Method	# LMI variables	# LMIs	stable
6 local models			
common quadratic	1	7	
fuzzy (all transitions)	6	42	
fuzzy (proposed method)	6	28	✓
5 local models			
common quadratic	1	6	
fuzzy (all transitions)	5	30	✓
fuzzy (proposed method)	5	22	✓
4 local models			
common quadratic	1	5	
fuzzy (all transitions)	4	20	✓
fuzzy (proposed method)	4	16	✓
3 local models			
common quadratic	1	3	
fuzzy (all transitions)	3	12	
fuzzy (proposed method)	3	10	✓

3.6 Example: Comparison of the Treated Lyapunov Approaches

For illustrative purposes the stability of a complex nonlinear dynamic process is investigated by using the presented Lyapunov approaches of Section 3.4 and using the transition determination of Section 3.5. By means of the decay rate and LMNs comprising different numbers of local models the conservatism of the considered Lyapunov approaches is compared and the influence of the transition determination is demonstrated.

The nonlinear dynamic process is adopted from [10], [61] and is described by the following difference equation:

$$y(k) = 0.133u(k-1) - 0.0677u(k-2) + 1.5y(k-1) \tag{3.74}$$
$$- 0.7y(k-2) + u(k)[0.1y(k-1) - 0.2y(k-2)] \tag{3.75}$$

In this example the input $u(k)$ is bounded to the interval $[-1.75,\ 0.5]$.

Figure 3.22 demonstrates that the system has weakly damped oscillatory behavior for large inputs whereas for small inputs strongly damped aperiodic behavior is present.

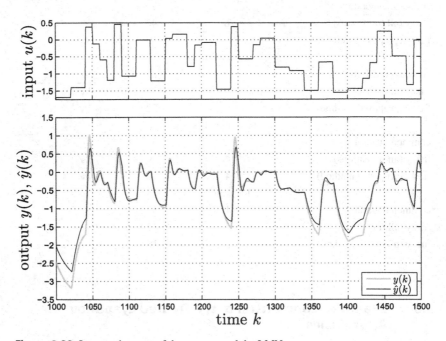

Figure 3.22 Input and output of the process and the LMN

For system identification an excitation signal was generated to capture both the nonlinear dynamic and static behavior, [56]. From these data different LMNs comprising up to eight local models were generated by the algorithm presented in [22], where the local models are defined by an axis oblique decomposition of the partition space. Figure 3.23 shows a contour plot of the validity functions

$$\tilde{x}(k) = [u(k-1)\ \hat{y}(k-1)] \tag{3.76}$$

as well as the identification data of the LMN with eight local models.

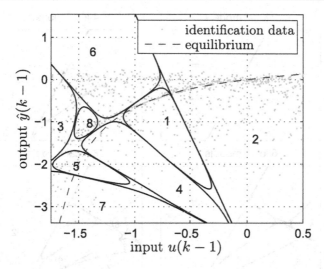

Figure 3.23 Contour plot of the validity functions and identification data sequence

The partitioning strategy in [22] uses statistical methods to avoid overfitting by local models generated with only few observations. Figure 3.24 illustrates a contour plot of the validity functions of LMNs comprising 2, 4, 6 and 8 local models.

Figure 3.25 illustrates the different decay rates determined by the three investigated Lyapunov based stability criteria depending on the number of local models.

This example shows noteworthy results:

- In all cases the fuzzy Lyapunov approach achieves the smallest decay rate and thus is the least conservative (excluding the piecewise quadratic Lyapunov approach without the upper bounds). This agrees with the results of [29, 31, 34, 44].
- There is no monotonic behavior of the different decay rates as the number of local models is increased. This is due to the fact that the difficulty of finding a suitable Lyapunov function mainly depends on the local dynamics *and* the number of LMIs. By increasing the number of local models the variety of the different local dynamics gradually decreases *and* the number of LMIs of the stability criteria is increased at the same time.

  The LMNs with less than four models are a coarse approximation of the process. This leads to strongly different dynamics of the local models and thus to high conservatism. The decrease of the conservatism observed when the number of

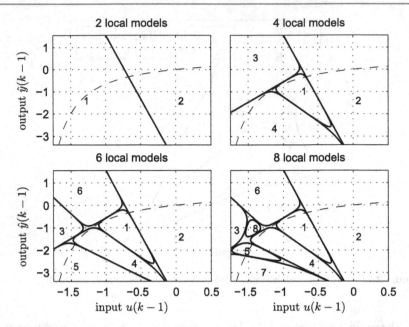

Figure 3.24 Contour plot of the validity functions of LMNs with different number of local models

local models is increased from four to six local models can be attributed to the reduced differences of the local system dynamics (compare Figure 3.24). For more than six models the conservatism grows in all approaches. Thus, for stability analysis of this example the optimal number of local models is six. Furthermore, this can be an important advantage for controller design because the optimal number of local models, and consequent local controllers can be a priori identified by the LMN with the smallest decay rate.

- There is a strong influence of the upper bounds to the conservatism of the piecewise quadratic Lyapunov approach (compare light-gray and white of Figure 3.25). This general relationship has already been mentioned in [29, 31, 50, 51]. Figure 3.25 further shows that the influence of the upper bounds is more dominant than the influence of the piecewise quadratic Lyapunov approach itself.

Using the algorithm presented in Section 3.5 the following model transitions (see (3.33) and (3.51)) are determined for the LMN comprising eight local models:

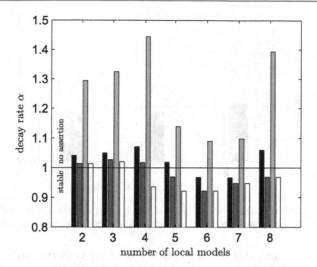

Figure 3.25 Minimum decay rate α of different stability criteria depending on the number of local models; common quadratic Lyapunov approach (black), fuzzy Lyapunov approach (dark gray), piecewise quadratic Lyapunov approach with upper bounds as in [50] (light gray), piecewise quadratic Lyapunov approach without upper bounds (for comparison) (white)

$$\Omega_1^p = \{1,\ 2,\ 6\},\ \ \Omega_2^p = \{1,\ 2\},$$
$$\Omega_3^p = \{3,\ 5,\ 8\},\ \ \Omega_4^p = \{1,\ 2,\ 4,\ 5,\ 6\},$$
$$\Omega_5^p = \{4,\ 5,\ 7\},\ \ \Omega_6^p = \{1,\ 3,\ 4,\ 6,\ 8\},\ \ \ \ \ \ \ (3.77)$$
$$\Omega_7^p = \{4,\ 5,\ 7\},\ \ \Omega_8^p = \{4,\ 5,\ 8\}$$

$$\Omega_1^f = \{1,\ 2,\ 4\ ,6\},\ \ \Omega_2^f = \{1,\ 2,\ 4\},$$
$$\Omega_3^f = \{3,\ 5,\ 6,\ 8\},\ \ \Omega_4^f = \{1,\ 2,\ 4,\ 5,\ 6,\ 7,\ 8\},$$
$$\Omega_5^f = \{3,\ 4,\ 5,\ 7,\ 8\},\ \ \Omega_6^f = \{1,\ 3,\ 4,\ 6,\ 8\},\ \ \ \ \ \ \ (3.78)$$
$$\Omega_7^f = \{4,\ 5,\ 7\},\ \ \Omega_8^f = \{3,\ 4,\ 5,\ 6,\ 8\}$$

Using (3.77) for the piecewise quadratic Lyapunov approach the number of LMIs in (3.32) can be reduced from 64 to 27. Using (3.78) for the fuzzy Lyapunov approach the number of LMIs in (3.50) can be reduced from 64 to 36.

Figure 3.26 illustrates the influence of the transition determination method of Section 3.5 by means of the fuzzy Lyapunov approach.

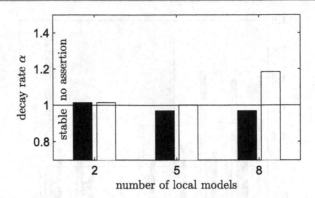

Figure 3.26 Minimum decay rate α of the fuzzy Lyapunov approach depending on the considered transitions; transition determination (3.78) (black), all transitions (3.52) (white)

Figure 3.26 shows that the potential to reduce the conservatism is increased by the number of local models. The transition determination cannot reduce the conservatism of an LMN with only two local models because there is no possibility to reduce the number of LMIs. For five local models a small but significant reduction of the transitions is achieved. Considering the LMN with eight local models it is apparent that a stability check without proper transition determination does not allow for an assertion.

Closed-Loop Stability Analysis and Controller Design

4

4.1 Introduction

LMNs approximate nonlinear plants as a weighted aggregation of some linear subsystems. Each linear subsystem models the dynamics of the nonlinear plant in a local operating area. Based on the LMN a nonlinear state-feedback controller can be designed. In literature there exist many approaches for the design of controllers for LMNs. An extensive overview is given in [43]. This chapter treats stability analysis of state-feedback controllers based on LMNs. Controllers for LMN mostly involve local controllers, each of which is assigned to a particular local model, yielding a so called local controller network (LCN), see Figure 4.1, [62].

This architecture is commonly known as **p**arallel **d**istributed **c**ompensator (PDC) which is based on the concept that for each local model (or fuzzy rule) one set of local controller parameters (or one local feedback controller) is used, as depicted in Figure 4.1. The global controller parameters are scheduled by the validity functions of the LMN.

As for the open loop Lyapunov approaches are most popular for stability analysis of control systems which are based on LMNs, see e.g. [36, 38, 45, 52, 53, 64, 65, 66, 67, 68]. However, this chapter presents two basic stability criteria for closed-loop systems which are based on the open loop stability criteria from Chapter 3:

Electronic supplementary material The online version of this chapter (https://doi.org/10.1007/978-3-658-34008-7_4) contains supplementary material, which is available to authorized users.

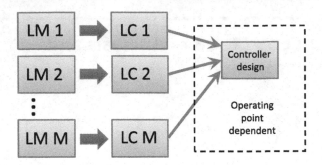

Figure 4.1 Local controller network, [63]

- Common quadratic Lyapunov approach
- Fuzzy Lyapunov approach

The Piecewise Quadratic Lyapunov approach is not considered for closed loop stability because of two reasons:

① Section 3.6 has shown that for discrete time systems the Piecewise Quadratic Lyapunov approach is more conservative than the other two approaches.

② In existing literature (e.g. [29, 31]) the Piecewise Quadratic Lyapunov approach is only used for systems with a constant input matrix. The input matrix of LMNs depends on the partition space (see 3.4.4) and is thus not constant.

Consequently, it is not to be expected that an extension of the existing Piecewise Quadratic Lyapunov approach for LMNs will give better results than the other two investigated Lyapunov approaches.

Controller design is an important issue in the field of systems and control. The goal of controller design is to determine a controller for a given system such that the closed loop is asymptotically or exponentially stable *and* satisfies specific requirements. For this purpose, the Lyapunov based stability criteria for the closed-loop are extended such that the feedback matrices can be calculated with state of the art LMI solvers. This enables state-feedback controller design for LMNs with guarantee stability. Further, it is shown how a weighting matrix can be determined to distribute the control effort between the inputs. Additionally, a feedforward controller can be designed to compensate measurable disturbances.

4.2 State-Feedback Control Law

The control law adopts the partitioning from the LMN and is as follows:

$$u(k) = \sum_{\mathcal{I}} \Phi_i(\tilde{x}(k))[-K_i x(k) + k_w^{(i)}(w(k) + w_o(k))], \tag{4.1}$$

where $w(k)$ is the reference signal and $w_o(k)$ is an optional offset to compensate measurable disturbance and the local affine term:

$$w_o(k) = w_z(k) + \sum_{\mathcal{I}} \Phi_i(\tilde{x}(k)) w_f^{(i)}, \tag{4.2}$$

where $w_f^{(i)}$ is for the local affine term and $w_z(k)$ is for the disturbances. Thus, the closed loop system consisting of the LMN and the smooth controller (4.1) can be described as:

$$
\begin{aligned}
x(k+1) &= \sum_{\mathcal{I}} \sum_{j \in \mathcal{I}} \Phi_i(\tilde{x}(k)) \Phi_j(\tilde{x}(k)) \Big[(A_i - B_i K_j) x(k) + f_i + \\
&\quad + B_i k_w^{(j)} (w(k) + w_z(k) + w_f^{(i)}) \Big] \\
&= \sum_{\mathcal{I}} \Phi_i(\tilde{x}(k))^2 [G_{ii} x(k) + f_i + B_i k_w^{(i)}(w(k) + w_z(k) + w_f^{(i)})] + \\
&\quad + 2 \sum_{i<j\leq l} \Phi_i(\tilde{x}(k)) \Phi_j(\tilde{x}(k)) \Big[\frac{G_{ij} + G_{ji}}{2} x(k) + f_i + \\
&\quad + B_i k_w^{(j)}(w(k) + w_z(k) + w_f^{(i)}) \Big] \\
&= \sum_{\mathcal{I}} \Phi_i^2 [\Lambda_{ii} x(k) + B_i k_w^{(i)}(w(k) + w_z(k) + w_f^{(i)})] + \\
&\quad + 2 \sum_{i<j\leq l} \Phi_i \Phi_j [\Lambda_{ij} x(k) + B_i k_w^{(j)}(w(k) + w_z(k) + w_f^{(i)})]
\end{aligned} \tag{4.3}
$$

with

$$G_{ij} = A_i - B_i K_j, \; i, j \in \mathcal{I} \tag{4.4}$$

$$\Lambda_{ii} = G_{ii}, \; i \in \mathcal{I} \tag{4.5}$$

$$\Lambda_{ij} = \frac{G_{ij} + G_{ji}}{2}, \; i < j \le I. \tag{4.6}$$

Remark 4.1 *For closed loop stability analysis by means of Lyapunov stability criteria only the feedback loop needs to be considered. Thus, both the reference $w(k)$ and the offset compensator $w_o(k)$ are assumed to be zero:*

$$w(k) \equiv 0, \; w_o(k) \equiv 0, \; \forall k \in \mathbb{N}^+$$

4.3   Local Model Network in State-Space Notation for Closed-Loop Stability Analysis and Controller Design

The considered state-feedback controllers for LMNs are known as parallel distributed compensators (PDC) and depicted in Figure 4.2.

A reasonable approach is to split the inputs of the LMN into inputs which are used for control:

$$\mathcal{P} \subseteq \mathcal{J} \tag{4.7}$$

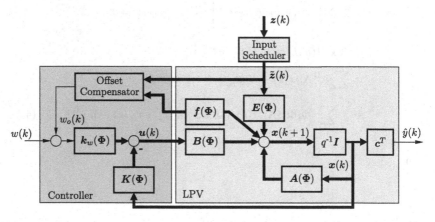

Figure 4.2 State-Space controller design for LMNs

and inputs which are considered as (measurable) disturbances:

$$\mathcal{R} = \mathcal{J} \setminus \mathcal{P} \tag{4.8}$$

As mentioned in Section 3.4.4 for closed loop stability analysis and controller design the state-space model must be different to the one in Section 3.4.4. The reason is that the input scheduler would highly increase the complexity of the closed loop. The advantage of the input scheduler approach is that a minimal state-space system can be used for open loop stability analysis. For the closed loop this advantage is void and a non-minimal state-space system is suitable. Thus the functionality of the input scheduler is integrated into the system matrix of the state-space system and the state vector gets the following form:

$$x(k) = \begin{pmatrix} u_{\mathcal{P}(1)}(k) \\ \vdots \\ u_{\mathcal{P}(|\mathcal{P}|)}(k) \\ \hat{y}(k-N+1) \\ \vdots \\ \hat{y}(k-1) \\ \hat{y}(k) \end{pmatrix}, \quad x \in \mathbb{R}^{\sum_{\mathcal{P}} M_{\mathcal{P}} - |\mathcal{P}| + N \times 1} \tag{4.9}$$

with

$$u_p(k) = \begin{pmatrix} u_p(k - M_{\mathcal{P}} + 1) \\ \vdots \\ u_p(k-1) \end{pmatrix}, \quad u_p \in \mathbb{R}^{M_p - 1 \times 1}, \ \forall p \in \mathcal{P} \tag{4.10}$$

The input vector $u(k)$ contains all inputs which are used for control:

$$u(k) = \begin{pmatrix} u_{\mathcal{P}(|\mathcal{P}|)}(k) \\ \vdots \\ u_{\mathcal{P}(1)}(k) \end{pmatrix}, \quad u \in \mathbb{R}^{|\mathcal{P}| \times 1} \tag{4.11}$$

The disturbance vector $\tilde{z}(k)$ contains all time shifted inputs which are not used for control and is provided by an input scheduler as described in Section 3.4.4:

$$\tilde{z}(k) = \begin{pmatrix} z_{\mathcal{R}(1)}(k) \\ \vdots \\ z_{\mathcal{R}(|\mathcal{R}|)}(k) \end{pmatrix}, \; \tilde{z} \in \mathbb{R}^{\sum_{\mathcal{R}} M_{\mathcal{R}} \times 1} \tag{4.12}$$

with

$$z_r(k) = \begin{pmatrix} u_r(k-1) \\ \vdots \\ u_r(k-M_{\mathcal{R}}) \end{pmatrix}, \; z_r \in \mathbb{R}^{M_r \times 1}, \; \forall r \in \mathcal{R} \tag{4.13}$$

The state-space system

$$x(k+1) = [A(\boldsymbol{\Phi}) - B(\boldsymbol{\Phi})K(\boldsymbol{\Phi})] x(k) +$$
$$+ B(\boldsymbol{\Phi})k_w(\boldsymbol{\Phi})(w(k) + w_o(k)) + E(\boldsymbol{\Phi})\tilde{z}(k) + f(\boldsymbol{\Phi}) \tag{4.14}$$
$$\hat{y}(k) = c^T x(k) \tag{4.15}$$

represents the LMN as described in Chapter 2 which is controlled by a state-feedback controller with the control law (4.1).

The matrices which describe the state-space system are as follows

$$A(\boldsymbol{\Phi}) = \sum_{\mathcal{I}} \Phi_i(\tilde{x}(k)) A_i, \; A \in \mathbb{R}^{\sum_{\mathcal{P}} M_{\mathcal{P}} - |\mathcal{P}| + N \times \sum_{\mathcal{P}} M_{\mathcal{P}} - |\mathcal{P}| + N} \tag{4.16}$$

$$B(\boldsymbol{\Phi}) = \sum_{\mathcal{I}} \Phi_i(\tilde{x}(k)) B_i, \; B \in \mathbb{R}^{\sum_{\mathcal{P}} M_{\mathcal{P}} - |\mathcal{P}| + N \times |\mathcal{P}|} \tag{4.17}$$

$$E(\boldsymbol{\Phi}) = \sum_{\mathcal{I}} \Phi_i(\tilde{x}(k)) E_i, \; E \in \mathbb{R}^{\sum_{\mathcal{P}} M_{\mathcal{P}} - |\mathcal{P}| + N \times \sum_{\mathcal{R}} |\mathcal{M}_{\mathcal{R}}|} \tag{4.18}$$

$$c^T = \begin{bmatrix} 0_{1 \times \sum_{\mathcal{P}} M_{\mathcal{P}} - |\mathcal{P}| + N - 1} & 1 \end{bmatrix}, \; c^T \in \mathbb{R}^{1 \times \sum_{\mathcal{P}} M_{\mathcal{P}} - |\mathcal{P}| + N} \tag{4.19}$$

$$K(\boldsymbol{\Phi}) = \sum_{\mathcal{I}} \Phi_i(\tilde{x}(k)) K_i, \; K^T \in \mathbb{R}^{|\mathcal{P}| \times \sum_{\mathcal{P}} M_{\mathcal{P}} + N} \tag{4.20}$$

$$k_w(\boldsymbol{\Phi}) = \sum_{\mathcal{I}} \Phi_i(\tilde{x}(k)) k_w^{(i)}, \; k_w \in \mathbb{R}^{|\mathcal{P}| \times 1} \tag{4.21}$$

The local system matrices A_i are as follows:

$$A_i = \begin{bmatrix} \underline{L}_{M_{\mathcal{P}(1)}} & & & \mathbf{0} \\ & \ddots & & \\ & & \underline{L}_{M_{\mathcal{P}(|\mathcal{P}|)}} & \\ \mathbf{0} & & & \overline{I}_N \\ \underline{b}_{\mathcal{P}(1)}^{(i)T} & \cdots & \underline{b}_{\mathcal{P}(|\mathcal{P}|)}^{(i)T} & a_i^T \end{bmatrix}, \ A \in \mathbb{R}^{\sum_{\mathcal{P}} M_{\mathcal{P}} - |\mathcal{P}| + N \times \sum_{\mathcal{P}} M_{\mathcal{P}} - |\mathcal{P}| + N}, \ \forall i \in \mathcal{I}$$

(4.22)

with

$$\underline{L}_m = \begin{cases} [\,] & m = 1 \\ \begin{bmatrix} \mathbf{0}_{m-2 \times 1} & I_{m-2} \\ \mathbf{0}_{1 \times m-1} \end{bmatrix} & \text{otherwise} \end{cases}, \ \underline{L}_m \in \mathbb{R}^{m-1 \times m-1}$$

$$\overline{I}_n = \begin{bmatrix} \mathbf{0}_{n-1 \times 1} & I_{n-1} \end{bmatrix}, \ \overline{I}_n \in \mathbb{R}^{n-1 \times n}$$

$$\underline{b}_p^{(i)T} = \begin{bmatrix} b_{p.M_p}^{(i)} & \cdots & b_{p.2}^{(i)} \end{bmatrix}, \ \underline{b}_p^{(i)T} \in \mathbb{R}^{1 \times M_p - 1}, \ \forall p \in \mathcal{P}, \ \forall i \in \mathcal{I}$$

$$a_i^T = \begin{bmatrix} a_N^{(i)} & \cdots & a_1^{(i)} \end{bmatrix}, \ a_i^T \in \mathbb{R}^{1 \times N}, \ \forall i \in \mathcal{I}.$$

The local input matrices B_i are as follows:

$$B_i = \begin{bmatrix} \overline{b}_{M_{\mathcal{P}(1)}} & & \mathbf{0} \\ & \ddots & \\ \mathbf{0} & & \overline{b}_{M_{\mathcal{P}(|\mathcal{P}|)}} \\ & \mathbf{0}_{N-1 \times |\mathcal{P}|} & \\ b_{\mathcal{P}(1).1}^{(i)} & \cdots & b_{\mathcal{P}(|\mathcal{P}|).1}^{(i)} \end{bmatrix}, \ B_i \in \mathbb{R}^{\sum_{\mathcal{P}} M_{\mathcal{P}} - |\mathcal{P}| + N \times |\mathcal{P}|}, \ \forall i \in \mathcal{I}$$

(4.23)

with

$$\overline{b}_m = \begin{bmatrix} \mathbf{0}_{m-1 \times 1} \\ 1 \end{bmatrix}, \ \overline{b}_m \in \mathbb{R}^{m \times 1}, \ \forall m \in \mathcal{M}_p, \ \forall p \in \mathcal{P}$$

The local disturbance matrices E_i are as follows:

$$E_i = \begin{bmatrix} \mathbf{0}_{\sum_{\mathcal{P}} M_{\mathcal{P}} - |\mathcal{P}| + N - 1 \times \sum_{\mathcal{R}} |\mathcal{M}_{\mathcal{R}}|} \\ b_{\mathcal{R}(1).1}^{(i)} & \cdots & b_{\mathcal{R}(|\mathcal{R}|).\mathcal{M}_{\mathcal{R}(|\mathcal{R}|)}}^{(i)} \end{bmatrix}, \ E_i \in \mathbb{R}^{\sum_{\mathcal{P}} M_{\mathcal{P}} - |\mathcal{P}| + N \times \sum_{\mathcal{R}} |\mathcal{M}_{\mathcal{R}}|}, \ \forall i \in \mathcal{I}$$

(4.24)

4.4 Closed-Loop Stability Analysis using the Common Quadratic Lyapunov Approach

The common quadratic Lyapunov approach for the closed loop follows the same concept as the approach of the open loop which is described in Section 3.4.5. Thus, the used Lyapunov function (3.23) is reviewed:

$$V(k) = \mathbf{x}^T(k)\mathbf{P}\mathbf{x}(k) > 0, \ \forall k \in \mathbb{N}^+$$

The common quadratic Lyapunov approach for closed loop stability analysis from [36, Theorem 8] is extended by the decay rate according to Lemma 3.1:

Theorem 4.1 *A LMN is exponentially stable in the large with the decay rate α if there exist symmetric matrices $\mathbf{P}$ and X_{ij} such that*

$$\mathbf{P} \succ 0 \tag{4.25}$$

$$\inf\left\{0 < \alpha < 1 : \mathbf{\Lambda}_{ii}^T \mathbf{P}\mathbf{\Lambda}_{ii} + X_{ii} \prec \alpha^2 \mathbf{P}\right\} \tag{4.26}$$

$$\inf\left\{0 < \alpha < 1 : \mathbf{\Lambda}_{ij}^T \mathbf{P}\mathbf{\Lambda}_{ij} + X_{ij} \preceq \alpha^2 \mathbf{P}\right\} \tag{4.27}$$

$$\tilde{X} \equiv \begin{pmatrix} X_{11} & X_{12} & \cdots & X_{1n} \\ X_{12} & X_{22} & \cdots & X_{2n} \\ \vdots & & \ddots & \vdots \\ X_{1n} & X_{2n} & \cdots & X_{nn} \end{pmatrix} \succ 0 \tag{4.28}$$

$$\forall i \in \mathcal{I}, \ \forall i < j \leq I$$

The proof of Theorem 4.1 is given in Appendix B.5.

Remark 4.2 *Because of matrix $\tilde{X}$ not all plant-controller combinations $(j - i)$ need to be stable. However, it is mandatory that the nominal combinations $(i - i)$ are stable to satisfy (4.28).*

4.5 Closed-Loop Stability Analysis using the Fuzzy Lyapunov Approach

The fuzzy Lyapunov approach for the closed loop follows the same concept as the approach of the open loop which is described in Section 3.4.10. Thus, the used Lyapunov function (3.48) is reviewed:

$$V(k) = x^T(k)\left(\sum_{\mathcal{I}} \Phi_i(\tilde{x}(k))P_i\right)x(k) > 0, \ \forall k \in \mathbb{N}^+$$

The fuzzy Lyapunov approach for closed loop stability analysis from [31, Theorem 5.8] is extended by the decay rate according to Lemma 3.1:

Theorem 4.2 *The equilibrium of the* discrete *fuzzy control system is exponentially stable in the large with the decay rate* α *if there exist symmetric matrices* P *and a set of matrices* $\Psi^l_{ij} = (\Psi^l_{ji})^T$, $i, j, l \in \mathcal{I}$, $i < j$ *such that*

$$P_i \succ 0, \ \forall i \in \mathcal{I} \tag{4.29}$$

$$\inf\left\{0 < \alpha < 1: \ \Lambda_{ij}^T P_j \Lambda_{ij} + \Psi^l_j \prec \alpha^2 P_l\right\}, \ \forall i, j, l \in \mathcal{I} \tag{4.30}$$

$$\inf\left\{0 < \alpha < 1: \ \Lambda_{ij}^T P_i \Lambda_{ij} + \Lambda_{ji}^T P_j \Lambda_{ji} + \Psi^l_{ij} + \Psi^l_{ji} \prec 2\alpha^2 P_l\right\}, \ \forall i, j, l \in \mathcal{I}, i < j \tag{4.31}$$

$$\Psi^l \equiv \begin{pmatrix} 2\Psi^l_1 & \Psi^l_{12} & \cdots & \Psi^l_{1I} \\ \Psi^l_{21} & 2\Psi^l_2 & \cdots & \Psi^l_{2I} \\ \vdots & & \ddots & \vdots \\ \Psi^l_{I1} & \Psi^l_{I2} & \cdots & 2\Psi^l_I \end{pmatrix} \succ 0, \ l \in \mathcal{I} \tag{4.32}$$

The proof of Theorem 4.2 follows from B.4 and B.5.

4.6   State-Space Controller Design using the Common Quadratic Lyapunov Approach

The common quadratic Lyapunov approach for state-space controller design from [36, Theorem 12] is extended by the decay rate according to Lemma 3.1:

Theorem 4.3 *The equilibrium of the dynamic LMN* (4.14) *is quadratically stabilizable via the fuzzy control law* (4.1) *in the large if there exist symmetric matrices* Q *and* Y_{ij} *and matrices* N_i *in such a way that*

$$Q \succ 0 \tag{4.33}$$

$$\begin{bmatrix} Q - Y_{ii} & QA_i^T - N_i^T B_i^T \\ A_i Q - B_i N_i & \alpha^2 Q \end{bmatrix} \succ 0 \tag{4.34}$$

$$\begin{bmatrix} Q - Y_{ij} & \frac{1}{2}(QA_i^T + QA_j^T - N_i^T B_j^T - N_j^T B_i^T) \\ \frac{1}{2}(A_i Q + A_j Q - B_i N_j - B_j N_i) & \alpha^2 Q \end{bmatrix} \succeq 0,$$

$$(4.35)$$

$$\forall i \in \mathcal{I}$$
$$\forall i < j \le I$$

$$\tilde{Y} \equiv \begin{pmatrix} Y_{11} & Y_{12} & \cdots & Y_{1I} \\ Y_{12} & Y_{22} & \cdots & Y_{2I} \\ \vdots & & \ddots & \vdots \\ Y_{1I} & Y_{2I} & \cdots & Y_{II} \end{pmatrix} \succ 0 \qquad (4.36)$$

In this case, the dynamic local feedback gains are

$$K_i = N_i Q^{-1}, \ \forall i \in \mathcal{I}. \qquad (4.37)$$

The proof of Theorem 4.3 directly follows from B.5, the Schur Complement (Lemma A.2) and the matrix transformation (4.37) and is thus omitted, [31].

4.7   State-Space Controller Design using the Fuzzy Lyapunov Approach

The fuzzy Lyapunov approach for state-space controller design from [31, Theorem 5.9] is extended by the decay rate according to Lemma 3.1:

Theorem 4.4 *The LMN (4.14) controlled via the fuzzy control law (4.1) is globally exponentially stable if there exists a set of positive definite matrices Q_i, $i \in \mathcal{I}$, two sets of matrices S_i, G_i, $i \in \mathcal{I}$, a set of symmetric matrices Φ_i^l, $i, l \in \mathcal{I}$, and a set of matrices $\Psi_{ij}^l = (\Psi_{ji}^l)^T$, $i, j, l \in \mathcal{I}$, $i < j$ and the decay rate α such that the following LMIs are satisfied,*

$$\begin{bmatrix} Q_j - G_j^T - G_j + \Psi_j^l & G_l^T A_j^T + S_j^T B_j^T \\ A_l G_j + B_j S_j & -\alpha^2 Q_l \end{bmatrix} \prec 0, \ j, l \in \mathcal{I} \qquad (4.38)$$

$$\begin{bmatrix} Q_i - G_j^T - G_j + \Psi_{ij}^l & G_l^T A_i^T + S_j^T B_i^T \\ A_i G_j + B_i S_j & -\alpha^2 Q_l \end{bmatrix} +$$

$$+ \begin{bmatrix} Q_j - G_i^T - G_i + \Psi_{ji}^l & G_l^T A_j^T + S_i^T B_j^T \\ A_j G_i + B_j S_i & -\alpha^2 Q_l \end{bmatrix} \prec 0, \ i, j, l \in \mathcal{I}, \ i < j \qquad (4.39)$$

$$\Psi^l \equiv \begin{pmatrix} 2\Psi_1^l & \Psi_{12}^l & \cdots & \Psi_{1I}^l \\ \Psi_{21}^l & 2\Psi_2^l & \cdots & \Psi_{2I}^l \\ \vdots & & \ddots & \vdots \\ \Psi_{I1}^l & \Psi_{I2}^l & \cdots & 2\Psi_I^l \end{pmatrix} \succ 0, \; l \in \mathcal{I} \qquad (4.40)$$

In this case, the local feedback gains are

$$K_i = S_i G_i^{-1}, \; \forall i \in \mathcal{I}. \qquad (4.41)$$

The proof of Theorem 4.4 directly follows from Theorem 4.2, B.5, the Schur Complement (Lemma A.2) and the matrix transformation (4.41) and is thus omitted, [31].

4.8 Optimal Input Gain and Offset Compensator Design

This section treats two topics:

① **Optimal gain matrix $k_w(k)$**
For LMNs with MISO (multiple input single output) structure it is reasonable to split the control effort between the inputs in an optimal way.

② **Offset Compensator**
The local affine term $f(\Phi)$ and the disturbances $\tilde{z}(k)$ are not considered by the state-feedback matrix of a state-feedback controller, see Figure 4.2. Thus, they cause a static offset of the output and a control error. A reasonable way to compensate this offset is to adapt the reference signal such that the influences of the disturbances and the local affine terms vanish.

The basic concept of this approach is to determine the local reference gain matrices k_i^w and aggregate them to the global one (PDC concept):

$$k_w(k) = k_w(\Phi) = \sum_{\mathcal{I}} \Phi_i(\tilde{x}(k))k_w^{(i)} \qquad (4.42)$$

Thus, the following local state-space system is suitable

$$x(k+1) = \sum_{\mathcal{I}} \Phi_i(\tilde{x}(k)) \left[A_i x(k) + B_i u_i(k) + E_i \tilde{z}(k) + f_i \right] \qquad (4.43)$$

$$y(k) = c^T x(k) \qquad (4.44)$$

to determine the local reference gain matrices $k_w^{(i)}$ as well as the offset compensator $w_o(k)$. The following local control law results from (4.1) and (4.2):

$$u_i(k) = -K_i x(k) + k_w^{(i)}(w(k) + w_z(k) + w_f^{(i)}), \quad \forall i \in \mathcal{I} \qquad (4.45)$$

Inserting (4.45) in (4.43):

$$x(k+1) = \sum_{\mathcal{I}} \Phi_i(\tilde{x}(k)) \left[(A_i - B_i K_i)x(k) + B_i k_w^{(i)}(w(k) + w_z(k) + w_f^{(i)}) + E_i \tilde{z}(k) + f_i \right] \qquad (4.46)$$

with $t \to \infty$ and assuming $w_{z,\infty} = w_z(k)$, $\tilde{z}_\infty = \tilde{z}(k)$ as follows:

$$x_\infty = \sum_{\mathcal{I}} \left[(I + B_i K_i - A_i)^{-1} B_i k_w^{(i)}(w_\infty + w_z(k) + w_f^{(i)}) + \right.$$
$$\left. + (I + B_i K_i - A_i)^{-1}(E_i \tilde{z}(k) + f_i) \right] \qquad (4.47)$$

$$y_\infty = \sum_{\mathcal{I}} \left[\underbrace{c^T(I + B_i K_i - A_i)^{-1} B_i}_{h_i^T} k_w^{(i)}(w_\infty + w_z(k) + w_f^{(i)}) + \right.$$
$$\left. + c^T(I + B_i K_i - A_i)^{-1}(E_i \tilde{z}(k) + f_i) \right] \qquad (4.48)$$

With $y_\infty = w_\infty$, satisfying (4.48) and the assumption, that w_z compensates the disturbances $\tilde{z}$, w_f compensates the local affine term f_i and $\tilde{z}(k) \equiv \tilde{z}_\infty$ follows:

$$w_\infty h_i^T k_w^{(i)} = w_\infty, \qquad \forall i \in \mathcal{I}, \qquad (4.49)$$

$$h_i^T k_w^{(i)} w_f^{(i)} + c^T(I + B_i K_i - A_i)^{-1} f_i = 0, \qquad \forall i \in \mathcal{I}, \qquad (4.50)$$

$$h^T(\Phi)k_w(\Phi)w_z(k) + c^T(I + B(\Phi)K(\Phi) - A(\Phi))^{-1}E(\Phi)\tilde{z}(k) = 0, \qquad \forall k \in \mathbb{N}^+. \qquad (4.51)$$

Thus,

$$h_i^T k_w^{(i)} = 1, \qquad \forall i \in \mathcal{I} \qquad (4.52)$$

$$w_f^{(i)} = -\frac{c^T(I + B_i K_i - A_i)^{-1} f_i}{h_i^T k_w^{(i)}}, \qquad \forall i \in \mathcal{I} \qquad (4.53)$$

$$w_z(k) = -\frac{c^T (I + B(\Phi)K(\Phi) - A(\Phi))^{-1} E(\Phi)\tilde{z}(k)}{h^T (\Phi)k_w(\Phi)}, \qquad \forall k \in \mathbb{N}^+ \qquad (4.54)$$

$k_w^{(i)}$ are $(|\mathcal{P}| \times 1)$-vectors, but only (4.52) is available for its determination. Thus, additional conditions are required for an explicit determination of $k_w^{(i)}$:

The stationary state of the vector of the control inputs follows from the control law (4.45):

$$u_{i,\infty} = -K_i x_\infty + k_w^{(i)} w_\infty, \ \forall i \in \mathcal{I}. \qquad (4.55)$$

Inserting (4.47) for x_∞ (4.55) becomes

$$u_{i,\infty} = \underbrace{(-K_i (I + B_i K_i - A_i)^{-1} B_i + I)}_{\Gamma_i} k_w^{(i)} w_\infty, \ \forall i \in \mathcal{I} \qquad (4.56)$$

Thus,

$$u_{i,\infty} = \Gamma_i k_w^{(i)} w_\infty, \ \forall i \in \mathcal{I}. \qquad (4.57)$$

For the explicit determination of the $k_w^{(i)}$ a second equation results from the requirement for the stationary state:

$$\min\{u_{i,\infty}^T R_i u_{i,\infty}\}, \ \forall i \in \mathcal{I} \qquad (4.58)$$

where R_i are user defined local weighting matrices.

Thus, the stationary state requires minimal control costs in sense of the quadratic quality criterion. Inserting (4.57) in (4.58) results in

$$\min\{k_w^{(i)T} \Gamma_i^T R_i \Gamma_i k_w^{(i)}\}, \ \forall i \in \mathcal{I} \qquad (4.59)$$

because (4.58) must be satisfied for all w_∞ and the side condition (4.52) is necessary. Building a Lagrange-function

$$\mathcal{L}_i(k_w^{(i)}, \lambda_i) = k_w^{(i)T} \Gamma_i^T R_i \Gamma_i k_w^{(i)} + \lambda_i (h_i^T k_w^{(i)} - 1), \ \forall i \in \mathcal{I}, \qquad (4.60)$$

and solving (4.60) for $k_w^{(i)}$

$$k_w^{(i)} = -(2\Gamma_i^T R_i \Gamma_i)^{-1} h_i \lambda_i, \ \forall i \in \mathcal{I}. \qquad (4.61)$$

the unknown multipliers λ_i of (4.61) must be calculated according to (4.60):

$$\lambda_i = -(h_i^T (\Gamma_i^T R_i \Gamma_i)^{-1} h_i)^{-1}, \ \forall i \in \mathcal{I}. \qquad (4.62)$$

With λ_i from (4.62) $k_w^{(i)}$ can be finally determined from (4.61):

$$k_w^{(i)} = (2\Gamma_i^T R_i \Gamma_i)^{-1} h_i (h_i^T (\Gamma_i^T R_i \Gamma_i)^{-1} h_i)^{-1}, \ \forall i \in \mathcal{I} \qquad (4.63)$$

Remark 4.3 *The gain matrix $k_w^{(i)}$ as well as the compensator for the local affine terms $w_f^{(i)}$ may be calculated offline according to (4.63) and (4.53), respectively, for the local models and are aggregated online. The disturbances $\tilde{z}(k)$ are basically unknown and thus it is necessary to calculate the compensator for the disturbances (4.54) in each timestep.*

PID Controller Design

5

5.1 Introduction

In control engineering PID controllers have a long history. Due to their simplicity, they are used for many applications although numerous advanced control techniques have been developed. Heuristic tuning methods such as Ziegler-Nichols [69], and self-tuning methods which are based on relay-feedback [70] or optimization [71] have been proposed for linear systems. However, conventional PID control may not perform satisfactorily for nonlinear systems, higher order and time-delay systems, [31, 72, 73]. Industrial processes are usually nonlinear and calibration engineers have to invest a lot of time and knowledge for the tuning of the PID parameters. Thus, a systematic approach will help calibration engineers to design PID controllers for nonlinear systems.

For a systematic controller design, it is reasonable to approximate the nonlinear process. In this context it is suitable to use LMNs, which makes the design of PID controllers for nonlinear systems easier or even possible.

In recent years, model-based controller design has become more important due to its capability of controlling nonlinear systems in a well defined way, e.g. [74, 75, 76, 77]. One of the most important aspects of controller design is closed loop stability. In numerous works of fuzzy PID controllers bounded-input bounded-output (BIBO) stability is considered by means of the small gain theorem, e.g. [78, 79, 80, 81, 82, 83, 84]. In contrast, many recent works of state-feedback controller design for fuzzy systems consider asymptotic or exponential stability by

Electronic supplementary material The online version of this chapter (https://doi.org/10.1007/978-3-658-34008-7_5) contains supplementary material, which is available to authorized users.

C. Mayr, *Stability Analysis and Controller Design of Local Model Networks*, https://doi.org/10.1007/978-3-658-34008-7_5

means of Lyapunov's direct method [28] (e.g. [36, 38, 45, 52, 53, 64, 65, 66, 67, 68]). However, when asymptotic or exponential stability of the closed loop is claimed BIBO stability may be insufficient. Thus, it is reasonable to adapt the methods of state-feedback controller design for PID controller design. An important aspect of Lyapunov based controller design methods is that they commonly do not consider closed loop performance. Further, it must be noted that Lyapunov stability criteria are inherently conservative and for some systems a stability proof or the controller design may become difficult.

The main contribution of this chapter is the PID controller design for nonlinear systems represented by LMNs. The three most important characteristics of the proposed approach are as follows:

①   The scheduling of the PID parameters is based on optimization.
②   Due to the use of a Lyapunov stability criterion, the closed loop is guaranteed asymptotically or exponentially stable.
③   The global performance of the closed loop is taken into account.

The basic concept of the proposed method is commonly known as paralleled distributed compensator (PDC), [38, 85]. In such specific controller architectures one local controller is designed for each local model and the scheduling is adopted from the LMN. The utilized LMN architecture [17] uses local linearizations of the process where the partitioning strategy is based on the Levenberg-Marquardt algorithm. Thus, the scheduling of the PID gains follows from an optimized approximation of the nonlinear process.

The Lyapunov based stability criterion is an important innovation to the existing works where BIBO stability is considered, e.g. [78, 79, 80, 81, 82, 83, 84]. Asymptotic or exponential stability as considered by Lyapunov methods are stronger than BIBO stability. Furthermore, a specific decay rate of the closed loop can be guaranteed or requested. The used Lyapunov based stability criterion is taken from [36], adapted for the considered closed loop system and extended by a decay rate. Here it must be noted, that Lyapunov based methods for controller design usually result in bilinear matrix inequalities (BMI) and cannot be solved by commonly used solvers for linear matrix inequalities (LMI) such as [47, 48, 49]. Solving such BMI means, that the Lyapunov function *and* the controller parameters are determined simultaneously. For common state-feedback controllers, a simple transformation is used to transform BMI into LMI, see e.g. [29, 36], Chapter 4. For PID controllers of LMN, such a transformation is not possible because of a rank deficiency caused by the limited controller parameters within the feedback matrix, [86]. Thus, two methods are proposed in this chapter for PID controller design by means of LMNs:

- iterative LMI (iLMI), [86].
- multi-objective genetic algorithm (multiGA) to handle the trade-off between stability and performance, [87].

The iterative method is introduced which uses a standard LMI solver. The basic concept is to determine *either* the Lyapunov function *or* the controller parameters in one iteration step. The used stability criterion is taken from [36], adapted for the considered closed loop system and extended by a decay rate to provide exponential stability as well as asymptotic stability. In contrast to the existing approach in [88] the presented method is an offline approach and thus needs less calculation effort during the control procedure. The method presented in [89] aims at robust PI controller design. However, a convergence of iLMI methods may not be guaranteed.

In [90], a method is introduced, which uses a Lyapunov based stability criterion. The main difference to the proposed approach is that local PID parameters are determined by means of linear control theory and the stability is subsequently determined by a Lyapunov stability criterion. Consequently, when the stability proof fails the PID controller design must be redone.

The basis for the proposed performance criterion is a reference sequence, which covers the whole operating area. This sequence is defined by Design of Experiments (DoE, [56]) to capture the whole nonlinear dynamic behavior of the closed loop. Based on the reference signal and commonly used parameters such as overshoot, rise time and settling time a non-penalty operating window for the output is defined. This is an important difference to [83] where a single reference step is used to minimize overshoot, settling time and the rise time of the output by means of a multiGA.

The PID parameters are determined by a multiGA [91, 92] where both *stability* and *performance* are considered. Thus, the proposed method offers the ability to handle the trade-off between *stability* and *performance*.

Both the local dynamics and the PID controllers are usually defined as transfer functions but Lyapunov stability criteria require state-space models. Thus, the closed loop, which consists of LMN and PID controllers, is transformed into a suitable state-feedback state-space system.

5.1.1   Discrete-time PID Control Algorithm

The discrete-time PID control law is as follows, [93]:

$$u(k) = K_P \left[e(k) + \frac{T_S}{T_N} \sum_{i=0}^{k-1} e(i) + \frac{T_V}{T_S} (e(k) - e(k-1)) \right] \quad (5.1)$$

where T_S denotes the sampling time and K_P, T_N and T_V are the controller parameters. The control error is

$$e(k) = w(k) - \hat{y}(k) \quad (5.2)$$

where $w(k)$ denotes the reference signal and $\hat{y}(k)$ is the (estimated) output. Rewriting (5.1) for $(k-1)$ and subtracting it from (5.1), one gets the PID control algorithm

$$u(k) = u(k-1) + d_0 e(k) + d_1 e(k-1) + d_2 e(k-2), \quad (5.3)$$

with the following coefficients:

$$d_0 = K_P \left[1 + \frac{T_V}{T_S} \right], \quad (5.4)$$

$$d_1 = K_P \left[\frac{T_S}{T_N} - \frac{2T_V}{T_S} - 1 \right], \quad (5.5)$$

$$d_2 = K_P \frac{T_V}{T_S}. \quad (5.6)$$

Eq. (5.3) can be reformulated by inserting (5.2) in (5.3)

$$u(k) = u(k-1) + \underbrace{\underbrace{k_{PID}^T(k) w(k)}_{v(k)} - k_{PID}^T(k) \hat{y}(k)}_{\Delta u(k)} \quad (5.7)$$

with

$$k_{PID}^T(k) = \left[d_2(k)\ d_1(k)\ d_0(k) \right], \quad \hat{y}(k) = \begin{bmatrix} \hat{y}(k-2) \\ \hat{y}(k-1) \\ \hat{y}(k) \end{bmatrix}, \quad w(k) = \begin{bmatrix} w(k-2) \\ w(k-1) \\ w(k) \end{bmatrix} \quad (5.8)$$

5.1.2 PID Control Algorithm for Local Model Networks

The basic concept of the proposed PID controller is commonly known as parallel distributed compensator (PDC), [38, 85, 94] where the scheduling is adopted from the LMN.

Remark 5.1 *The proposed method allows a simultaneous determination of multiple PID controllers where each controller uses one input as actuating value and all controllers control the same value (= system output, $\hat{y}(k)$). Further, the PID controllers do not have an interconnection. Nevertheless, stability issues should not arise because of the stability criterion within the design process. The application of parallel PID controllers for the same output is not common but exists in some industrial applications. The intake manifold pressure control for internal combustion engines is such a case. The intake manifold pressure may be simultaneously influenced by a turbo charger and the exhaust gas recirculation (EGR) rate where both variables are controlled with nonlinear PID controllers. The closed loop stability of such systems is usually crucial and the proposed method allows a systematic approach where stability is considered.*

To provide the ability of designing multiple PID controllers the set

$$\mathcal{P} \subseteq \mathcal{J} \tag{5.9}$$

contains all input indices where a PID controller acts. Consequently the set

$$\mathcal{R} = \mathcal{J} \setminus \mathcal{P} \tag{5.10}$$

contains all input indices which are not used to control the output. With (5.9) and (5.10) the system inputs are formally split into control inputs $u(k)$ and disturbances $z(k)$ as proposed in Section 4.2:

$$u(k) = \begin{bmatrix} u_{\mathcal{P}(1)}(k) \\ \vdots \\ u_{\mathcal{P}(|\mathcal{P}|)}(k) \end{bmatrix}, \ u(k) \in \mathbb{R}^{|\mathcal{P}| \times 1} \tag{5.11}$$

$$z(k) = \begin{bmatrix} u_{\mathcal{R}(1)}(k) \\ \vdots \\ u_{\mathcal{R}(|\mathcal{R}|)}(k) \end{bmatrix}, \ z(k) \in \mathbb{R}^{|\mathcal{R}| \times 1} \tag{5.12}$$

The basic concept of the proposed PID controller with selected inputs for control is depicted in Figure 5.1.

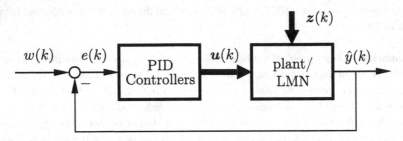

Figure 5.1 Concept of PID Controller for MISO Systems

The PID control law follows by extending the discrete-time PID law (5.7) as follows:

$$u(k) = u(k-1) + \underbrace{\underbrace{K_{PID}(k)w(k)}_{v(k)} - K_{PID}(k)\hat{y}(k)}_{\Delta u(k)} \qquad (5.13)$$

with

$$\Delta u(k) = \begin{bmatrix} \Delta u_{\mathcal{P}(1)}(k) \\ \vdots \\ \Delta u_{\mathcal{P}(|\mathcal{P}|)}(k) \end{bmatrix}, \quad \Delta u(k) \in \mathbb{R}^{|\mathcal{P}| \times 1}$$

$$K_{PID}(k) = \begin{bmatrix} d_{\mathcal{P}(1).2}(k) & d_{\mathcal{P}(1).1}(k) & d_{\mathcal{P}(1).0}(k) \\ & \vdots & \\ d_{\mathcal{P}(|\mathcal{P}|).2}(k) & d_{\mathcal{P}(|\mathcal{P}|).1}(k) & d_{\mathcal{P}(|\mathcal{P}|).0}(k) \end{bmatrix}, \quad K_{PID} \in \mathbb{R}^{|\mathcal{P}| \times 3}$$

In view of the actual nonlinear system which the LMN is supposed to represent, the local model partitioning represents a meaningful scheduling strategy. In this context there is an associated set of PID parameters $K_{PID}^{(i)}$ for each local model. The PID parameter sets results to the global time-varying matrix $K_{PID}(k)$ from aggregation:

$$K_{PID}(k) = K_{PID}(\Phi(\tilde{x}(k))) = \sum_{\mathcal{I}} \Phi_i(\tilde{x}(k)) K_{PID}^{(i)} \qquad (5.14)$$

with

$$K^{(i)}_{PID} = \begin{bmatrix} d^{(i)}_{\mathcal{P}(1).2} & d^{(i)}_{\mathcal{P}(1).1} & d^{(i)}_{\mathcal{P}(1).0} \\ & \vdots & \\ d^{(i)}_{\mathcal{P}(|\mathcal{P}|).2} & d^{(i)}_{\mathcal{P}(|\mathcal{P}|).1} & d^{(i)}_{\mathcal{P}(|\mathcal{P}|).0} \end{bmatrix}, \; K^{(i)}_{PID} \in \mathbb{R}^{|\mathcal{P}| \times 3}, \; \forall i \in \mathcal{I}$$

From (5.14) it becomes obvious that the PID parameters are varying with the premise vector $\tilde{x}(k)$.

5.2 Closed-Loop in State-Space Notation

In this section a state-space model is introduced which describes the closed loop according to Figure 5.1. A state-space description of the closed loop is required because a Lyapunov based stability analysis method is involved in the controller design method. The obtained state-space model is depicted in Figure 5.2 and provides equivalence between transfer function and the state-space system locally as well as in all interpolation regimes (globally). The split of the LMN inputs $u_{\mathcal{J}}$ into control inputs u and disturbances z allows that the time shifted signals of the disturbances are provided externally by the "Input Scheduler". This allows that the number of states in the state-space system is kept as small as possible; only the time shifts of the control inputs and the system output are created by the system matrix. However, due to the time shifted inputs within the state vector, the proposed system is a non-minimal state-space system. For the proposed PID controller design the non-minimal state-space system is not an issue, although state-feedback controller design for non-minimal state-space system may become problematic because of non-controllable states. This state-space system can be seen as a mixed notion of the open- and the closed loop state-space models, see Section 3.4.4, 4.3.

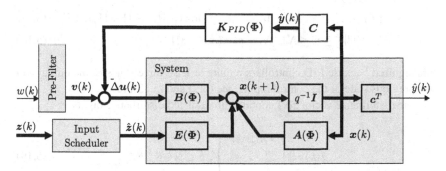

Figure 5.2 LMN with PID controller in state-space notation

5.2.1   Basic Concept

According to Figure 5.2 and (5.13) the PID control law is divided into three parts:

①   past inputs $u(k-1)$ (integrator)
②   "filtered" reference signals $v(k)$
③   feedback $K_{PID}(\Phi)\hat{y}(k)$

First, the state vector $x(k)$ is defined such that it contains time shifted values of the control inputs and time shifted values of the output as follows:

$$x(k) = \begin{pmatrix} u_{\mathcal{P}(1)}(k) \\ \vdots \\ u_{\mathcal{P}(|\mathcal{P}|)}(k) \\ \hline \hat{y}(k-\hat{N}+1) \\ \vdots \\ \hat{y}(k-1) \\ \hat{y}(k) \end{pmatrix}, \; x \in \mathbb{R}^{\sum_{\mathcal{P}} \hat{M}_{\mathcal{P}} + \hat{N} \times 1} \tag{5.15}$$

with

$$u_p(k) = \begin{pmatrix} u_p(k-\hat{M}_{\mathcal{P}}) \\ \vdots \\ u_p(k-1) \end{pmatrix}, \; u_p \in \mathbb{R}^{\hat{M}_p \times 1}, \; \forall p \in \mathcal{P} \tag{5.16}$$

where the modified sets

$$\hat{\mathcal{M}}_{\mathcal{P}} = \{\hat{m}_{\mathcal{P}} \in \mathbb{N} | 1 \le \hat{m}_{\mathcal{P}} \le \hat{M}_{\mathcal{P}}\}, \; \hat{M}_{\mathcal{P}} = \max(\{M_{\mathcal{P}}-1\} \cup \{1\}), \; \forall \mathcal{P} \tag{5.17}$$

$$\hat{\mathcal{N}} = \{\hat{n} \in \mathbb{N} | 1 \le \hat{n} \le \hat{N}\}, \; \hat{N} = \max(\mathcal{N} \cup \{3\}) \tag{5.18}$$

are required because PID controllers require at least three states of the output and the previous state of the control inputs, see (5.7) and (5.13), respectively.

The disturbance vector $\hat{z}(k)$ contains time shifted disturbance inputs

$$\hat{z}(k) = \begin{pmatrix} \hat{z}_{\mathcal{R}(1)}(k) \\ \vdots \\ \hat{z}_{\mathcal{R}(|\mathcal{R}|)}(k) \end{pmatrix}, \; \hat{z} \in \mathbb{R}^{\sum_{\mathcal{R}} \hat{M}_{\mathcal{R}} \times 1} \tag{5.19}$$

with

$$\hat{z}_r(k) = \begin{pmatrix} z_r(k - \hat{M}_r) \\ \vdots \\ z_r(k - 1) \end{pmatrix}, \ \hat{z}_r \in \mathbb{R}^{\hat{M}_r \times 1}, \ \forall r \in \mathcal{R} \tag{5.20}$$

and is provided by the so called "Input Scheduler", see Figure 5.2. Thus, the state-space system

$$x(k + 1) = A(\Phi)x(k) + B(\Phi)\Delta u(k) + E(\Phi)\hat{z}(k) \tag{5.21}$$

$$\hat{y}(k) = c^T x(k) \tag{5.22}$$

is equivalent to the PID controlled LMN as described in Section 2.2 and 5.1.2.

The matrices that describe the state-space system are as follows:

$$A(\Phi) = \sum_{\mathcal{I}} \Phi_i(\tilde{x}(k))A_i, \ A \in \mathbb{R}^{\sum_{\mathcal{P}} \hat{M}_{\mathcal{P}} + \hat{N} \times \sum_{\mathcal{P}} \hat{M}_{\mathcal{P}} + \hat{N}} \tag{5.23}$$

$$B(\Phi) = \sum_{\mathcal{I}} \Phi_i(\tilde{x}(k))B_i, \ B \in \mathbb{R}^{\sum_{\mathcal{P}} \hat{M}_{\mathcal{P}} + \hat{N} \times |\mathcal{P}|} \tag{5.24}$$

$$E(\Phi) = \sum_{\mathcal{I}} \Phi_i(\tilde{x}(k))E_i, \ E \in \mathbb{R}^{\sum_{\mathcal{P}} \hat{M}_{\mathcal{P}} + \hat{N} \times \sum_{\mathcal{R}} |\mathcal{M}_{\mathcal{R}}|} \tag{5.25}$$

$$c^T = \begin{bmatrix} 0_{1 \times \sum_{\mathcal{P}} \hat{M}_{\mathcal{P}} + \hat{N} - 1} & 1 \end{bmatrix}, \ c^T \in \mathbb{R}^{1 \times \sum_{\mathcal{P}} \hat{M}_{\mathcal{P}} + \hat{N}} \tag{5.26}$$

5.2.2   Construction of the System Matrices

Rewriting (2.14) for $(k + 1)$:

$$\hat{y}_i(k + 1) = \sum_{\mathcal{J}} \sum_{\mathcal{M}_{\mathcal{J}}} u_j(k - m_j + 1)b_{j.m_j}^{(i)} + \sum_{\mathcal{N}} \hat{y}(k - n + 1)a_n^{(i)} \tag{5.27}$$

and inserting $u(k)$ for the inputs which are used for PID control of (5.13) in (5.27) and by using the stets $\mathcal{P}$, $\mathcal{R}$, $\hat{M}_{\mathcal{P}}$, $\hat{N}$ the outputs of the local models are as follows:

$$\hat{y}_i(k+1) = \sum_{\mathcal{P}} u_{\mathcal{P}}(k-1)(b^{(i)}_{\mathcal{P}.1} + b^{(i)}_{\mathcal{P}.2}) + \Delta u_{\mathcal{P}}(k)b^{(i)}_{\mathcal{P}(|P|).1}$$

$$+ \sum_{m \in \hat{\mathcal{M}}_p \backslash \{1,2\}} u_{\mathcal{P}}(k-m+1)b^{(i)}_{\mathcal{P}.m} \tag{5.28}$$

$$+ \sum_{\mathcal{R}} \sum_{\mathcal{M}_{\mathcal{R}}} u_{\mathcal{R}}(k-m+1)b^{(i)}_{\mathcal{R}.\mathcal{M}_{\mathcal{R}}} + \sum_{\mathcal{N}} \hat{y}(k-n+1)a^{(i)}_n$$

The local system matrices A_i are as follows:

$$A_i = \begin{bmatrix} \underline{I}_{\hat{M}_{\mathcal{P}(1)}} & & & & 0 \\ & \ddots & & & \\ & & \underline{I}_{\hat{M}_{\mathcal{P}(|\mathcal{P}|)}} & & \\ 0 & & & \bar{I}_{\hat{N}} \\ \underline{b}^{(i)T}_{\mathcal{P}(1)} & \cdots & \underline{b}^{(i)T}_{\mathcal{P}(|\mathcal{P}|)} & a^T_i \end{bmatrix}, \quad A \in \mathbb{R}^{\sum_{\mathcal{P}} \hat{M}_{\mathcal{P}} + \hat{N} \times \sum_{\mathcal{P}} \hat{M}_{\mathcal{P}} + \hat{N}} \tag{5.29}$$

with

$$\underline{I}_m = \begin{bmatrix} 0_{m-1 \times 1} & I_{m-1} \\ 0_{1 \times m-1} & 1 \end{bmatrix}, \quad \underline{I}_m \in \mathbb{R}^{m \times m}$$

$$\bar{I}_n = \begin{bmatrix} 0_{n-1 \times 1} & I_{n-1} \end{bmatrix}, \quad \bar{I}_n \in \mathbb{R}^{n-1 \times n}$$

$$\underline{b}^{(i)T}_p = \begin{bmatrix} b^{(i)}_{p.\hat{M}_p+1} & \cdots & b^{(i)}_{p.3} & b^{(i)}_{p.2} + b^{(i)}_{p.1} \end{bmatrix}, \quad \underline{b}^{(i)T}_p \in \mathbb{R}^{1 \times \hat{M}_p}, \quad \forall p \in \mathcal{P}$$

$$a^T_i = \begin{bmatrix} a^{(i)}_{\hat{N}} & \cdots & a^{(i)}_1 \end{bmatrix}, \quad a^T_i \in \mathbb{R}^{1 \times \hat{N}}, \quad \forall i \in \mathcal{I}$$

$$\forall \hat{m}_p \in \hat{\mathcal{M}}_p \backslash \mathcal{M}_p : b^{(i)}_{p.\hat{m}_p} = 0, \quad \forall \hat{n} \in \hat{\mathcal{N}} \backslash \mathcal{N} : a^{(i)}_{\hat{n}} = 0$$

Remark 5.2 *To provide a feedback matrix with only three columns the feedback loop of the inputs $u_{\mathcal{P}}(k-1)$ is integrated in the system matrix. Thus, in $\underline{I}_n$ the last element is 1 and the last element of $\underline{b}^{(i)T}_p$ is $b^{(i)}_{p.2} + b^{(i)}_{p.1}$.*

The local input matrices B_i are as follows:

$$B_i = \begin{bmatrix} \overline{b}_{\hat{M}_{\mathcal{P}(1)}} & & & \mathbf{0} \\ & \ddots & & \\ \mathbf{0} & & \overline{b}_{\hat{M}_{\mathcal{P}(|\mathcal{P}|)}} & \\ & & \mathbf{0}_{\hat{N}-1\times|\mathcal{P}|} & \\ b^{(i)}_{\mathcal{P}(1).1} & \cdots & b^{(i)}_{\mathcal{P}(|\mathcal{P}|).1} & \end{bmatrix}, \; B_i \in \mathbb{R}^{\sum_{\mathcal{P}} \hat{M}_{\mathcal{P}}+\hat{N}\times|\mathcal{P}|} \qquad (5.30)$$

with

$$\overline{b}_m = \begin{bmatrix} \mathbf{0}_{m-1\times 1} \\ 1 \end{bmatrix}, \; \overline{b}_m \in \mathbb{R}^{m\times 1}$$

The local disturbance matrices E_i are as follows:

$$E_i = \begin{bmatrix} \mathbf{0}_{\sum_{\mathcal{P}} \hat{M}_{\mathcal{P}}+\hat{N}-1\times\sum_{\mathcal{R}}|\mathcal{M}_{\mathcal{R}}|} \\ b^{(i)}_{\mathcal{R}(1).1} \cdots b^{(i)}_{\mathcal{R}(|\mathcal{R}|).\mathcal{M}_{\mathcal{R}(|\mathcal{R}|)}} \end{bmatrix}, \; E_i \in \mathbb{R}^{\sum_{\mathcal{P}} \hat{M}_{\mathcal{P}}+\hat{N}\times\sum_{\mathcal{R}}|\mathcal{M}_{\mathcal{R}}|} \qquad (5.31)$$

Remark 5.3 *The notation of A_i according to (5.29), B_i according to (5.30) and E_i according to (5.31) guarantees that (5.28) with an inserted (2.14) and the last row of (3.13) are equal.*

5.2.3 Feedback Loop

The input vector $\hat{y}(k)$ of the feedback matrix is calculated as follows:

$$\hat{y}(k) = Cx(k) \qquad (5.32)$$

with

$$C = \begin{bmatrix} \mathbf{0}_{3\times\sum_{\mathcal{P}} \hat{M}_{\mathcal{P}}+\hat{N}-3} & I_3 \end{bmatrix}, \; C \in \mathbb{R}^{3\times\sum_{\mathcal{P}} \hat{M}_{\mathcal{P}}+\hat{N}}$$

5.3 Stability Criterion

The following criterion is based on Theorem 4.1, adapted for the considered closed loop system. Thus, it provides a statement on exponential stability of a PID controlled LMN, [95]:

Theorem 5.1 *The equilibrium of the PID controlled dynamic LMN (2.14) is exponentially stable via the control law (5.7) in the large if there exist symmetric matrices P and X_{ij} and a decay rate α such that*

$$P \succ 0 \tag{5.33}$$

$$\inf \left\{ 0 < \alpha < 1 : \Lambda_{ii}^T P \Lambda_{ii}^T + X_{ii} \prec \alpha^2 P \right\} \tag{5.34}$$

$$\inf \left\{ 0 < \alpha < 1 : \Lambda_{ij}^T P \Lambda_{ij}^T + X_{ij} \preceq \alpha^2 P \right\} \tag{5.35}$$

$$\tilde{X} = \begin{pmatrix} X_{11} & X_{12} & \cdots & X_{1I} \\ X_{12} & X_{22} & \cdots & X_{2I} \\ \vdots & & \ddots & \vdots \\ X_{1I} & X_{2I} & \cdots & X_{II} \end{pmatrix} \succ 0 \tag{5.36}$$

$$\forall i \in \mathcal{I}, \ \forall i < j \leq I$$

with

$$\Lambda_{ii} = G_{ii}, \ \Lambda_{ij} = \frac{G_{ij} + G_{ji}}{2},$$
$$G_{ij} = A_i - B_i K_{PID}^{(j)} C. \tag{5.37}$$

The proof of Theorem 5.1 directly follows from Proof B.5 and $K_i \equiv K_{PID}^{(i)} C$.

Remark 5.4 *There exist more advanced Lyapunov function candidates such as the fuzzy Lyapunov functions, see Section 4.7. The main drawback of such criteria is their bigger calculation effort, which becomes a particular problem when such stability criteria are combined with evolutionary algorithms or the iLMI method.*

Remark 5.5 *For unknown controller parameters a bilinear matrix inequality (BMI) arises from the product of P and $K_{PID}^{(i)}$ which results from inserting (5.37) in (5.34), (5.35), respectively. Such BMI are not solvable with state of the art LMI solvers. The feedback matrix of common state-feedback controllers may be directly determined by LMI solvers by means of a matrix transformation, see Sections 4.6 and 4.7. Due to the rank deficiency caused by the matrix C such a transformation is not possible for the introduced state-space system. Instead, in the proposed method the controller parameters are determined by the iLMI procedure of section 5.4.1 or multiGA presented in Section 5.4.2.*

5.4   Controller Design

The main issue of controller design using a Lyapunov based method is the fact that the LMIs of Theorem 5.1 become BMIs when the local feedback matrices $K_{PID}^{(i)}$ are unknown. BMIs are not solvable with LMI solvers. Further, the variable transformation of Theorem 4.3 where a new matrix variable is introduced is not possible for PID controllers. The reason is the rank deficiency of the feedback loop.

5.4.1   iLMI Procedure

Due to the fact that the BMIs of Theorem 5.1 are not solvable by state of the art LMI solvers an iterative method is introduced (iLMI). The basic idea is to use *either* the parameters of the Lyapunov function *or* the PID parameters as decision variables

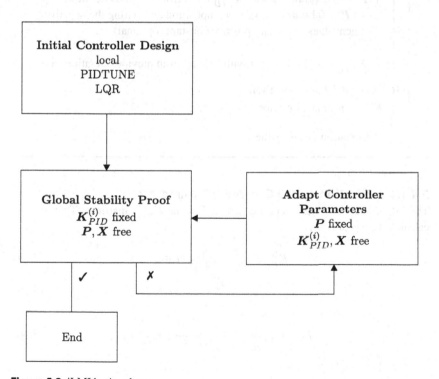

Figure 5.3 iLMI basic scheme

for the LMI solver in one iteration step. The remaining parameters are fixed as calculated in the previous iteration step. The basic concept of the iLMI procedure is illustrated in Figure 5.3.

The iLMI method described as pseudocode is as follows:

Algorithm 1: iLMI
---

begin
  Initial Design:
  set $K_{PID}^{(i)}$, $\forall i \in \mathcal{I}$ by an arbitrary method
  e.g.: local tuning, LQR, random
  $k \leftarrow 0$
  Iterative LMI design:
  while $k \leq k_{max}$ || *Theorem 5.1 is satisfied* **do**
    $k \leftarrow k + 1$
    if k *is odd* **then**
      $P \leftarrow$ Theorem 5.1 with $K_{PID}^{(i)}$ fixed from previous iteration step
      set $P \succ 0$ by using eigendecomposition and setting the negative
      eigenvalues to a small positive constant (optional)
    else
      $K_{PID}^{(i)} \leftarrow$ Theorem 5.1 with P fixed from previous iteration step

  if *Theorem 5.1 satisfied* **then**
    $K_{PID}^{(i)}$ from last iteration may be used
  else
    stabilization not possible

5.4.1.1 Limitation of PID Controller Parameters

The PID controller parameters are included in the $K_{PID}^{(i)}$ matrices. They can be calculated according to:

$$K_P^{(i)} = d_0^{(i)} - d_2^{(i)}, \ \forall i \in \mathcal{I} \tag{5.38}$$

$$T_V^{(i)} = T_S \frac{d_2^{(i)}}{d_0^{(i)} - d_2^{(i)}}, \ \forall i \in \mathcal{I} \tag{5.39}$$

$$T_N^{(i)} = T_S \frac{d_0^{(i)} - d_2^{(i)}}{d_0^{(i)} + d_1^{(i)} + d_2^{(i)}}, \ \forall i \in \mathcal{I} \tag{5.40}$$

with the following abbreviations

$$\Delta = \begin{bmatrix} -1 \\ 0 \\ 1 \end{bmatrix}, \quad \Gamma = \begin{bmatrix} 1 \\ 0 \\ 0 \end{bmatrix}, \quad \Upsilon = \begin{bmatrix} 1 \\ 1 \\ 1 \end{bmatrix}, \tag{5.41}$$

equations (5.38), (5.39) and (5.40) can be reformulated as follows:

$$K_P^{(i)} = K_{PID}^{(i)} \cdot \Delta, \ \forall i \in \mathcal{I} \tag{5.42}$$

$$T_V^{(i)} = T_S \frac{K_{PID}^{(i)} \Gamma}{K_{PID}^{(i)} \Delta}, \ \forall i \in \mathcal{I} \tag{5.43}$$

$$T_N^{(i)} = T_S \frac{K_{PID}^{(i)} \Delta}{K_{PID}^{(i)} \Upsilon}, \ \forall i \in \mathcal{I} \tag{5.44}$$

Since the LMI solvers require symmetric matrices all limitations have to be formulated as symmetric LMIs.

Imposing Constraints on $K_P^{(i)}$

Theorem 5.2 *The local gain $K_P^{(i)}$ of the PID controllers can be limited by the following inequality:*

$$K_{P,min}^{(i)} < \frac{1}{2} \cdot \left(K_{PID}^{(i)} \cdot \Delta + \Delta^T \cdot K_{PID}^{(i)T} \right) < K_{P,max}^{(i)}, \ \forall i \in \mathcal{I} \tag{5.45}$$

The proof of Theorem 5.2 is given in B.6

Imposing Constraints on $T_V^{(i)}$

Theorem 5.3 *The local $T_V^{(i)}$ of the PID controllers can be limited by the following inequalities:*

$$T_S \left(K_{PID}^{(i)} \Gamma + \Gamma^T K_{PID}^{(i)T} \right) < \begin{cases} T_{V,max}^{(i)} \left(K_{PID}^{(i)} \cdot \Delta + \Delta^T \cdot K_{PID}^{(i)T} \right) & \text{if } \mathrm{sign}(K_{PID}^{(i)} \cdot \Delta) = 1 \\ T_{V,min}^{(i)} \left(K_{PID}^{(i)} \cdot \Delta + \Delta^T \cdot K_{PID}^{(i)T} \right) & \text{if } \mathrm{sign}(K_{PID}^{(i)} \cdot \Delta) = -1 \end{cases},$$
$$\forall i \in \mathcal{I} \tag{5.46}$$

$$T_S \left(K_{PID}^{(i)} \Gamma + \Gamma^T K_{PID}^{(i)T} \right) > \begin{cases} T_{V,min}^{(i)} \left(K_{PID}^{(i)} \cdot \Delta + \Delta^T \cdot K_{PID}^{(i)T} \right) & \text{if } \mathrm{sign}(K_{PID}^{(i)} \cdot \Delta) = 1 \\ T_{V,max}^{(i)} \left(K_{PID}^{(i)} \cdot \Delta + \Delta^T \cdot K_{PID}^{(i)T} \right) & \text{if } \mathrm{sign}(K_{PID}^{(i)} \cdot \Delta) = -1 \end{cases},$$
$$\forall i \in \mathcal{I} \tag{5.47}$$

The proof of Theorem 5.3 is given in B.7.

Imposing Constraints on $T_N^{(i)}$

Theorem 5.4 *The local $T_N^{(i)}$ of the PID controllers can be limited by the following inequalities:*

$$T_S \left(K_{PID}^{(i)} \Delta + \Delta^T K_{PID}^{(i)T} \right) < \begin{cases} T_{N,max}^{(i)} \left(K_{PID}^{(i)} \cdot \Upsilon + \Upsilon^T \cdot K_{PID}^{(i)T} \right) & if \ \mathrm{sign}(K_{PID}^{(i)} \cdot \Upsilon) = 1 \\ T_{N,min}^{(i)} \left(K_{PID}^{(i)} \cdot \Upsilon + \Upsilon^T \cdot K_{PID}^{(i)T} \right) & if \ \mathrm{sign}(K_{PID}^{(i)} \cdot \Upsilon) = -1 \end{cases},$$
$$\forall i \in \mathcal{I} \tag{5.48}$$

$$T_S \left(K_{PID}^{(i)} \Delta + \Delta^T K_{PID}^{(i)T} \right) > \begin{cases} T_{N,min}^{(i)} \left(K_{PID}^{(i)} \cdot \Upsilon + \Upsilon^T \cdot K_{PID}^{(i)T} \right) & if \ \mathrm{sign}(K_{PID}^{(i)} \cdot \Upsilon) = 1 \\ T_{N,max}^{(i)} \left(K_{PID}^{(i)} \cdot \Upsilon + \Upsilon^T \cdot K_{PID}^{(i)T} \right) & if \ \mathrm{sign}(K_{PID}^{(i)} \cdot \Upsilon) = -1 \end{cases},$$
$$\forall i \in \mathcal{I} \tag{5.49}$$

The proof of Theorem 5.4 is given in B.8.

5.4.1.2 Example: Wiener Model, [95]

A stable second order Wiener model is considered. It consists of a dynamic linear block with a normalized transfer function $G_L(z) = V(z)/U(z)$ in cascade with a static nonlinearity $f(v)$ at the output with v as the intermediate variable at the output of the linear block, see 5.4.

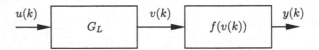

Figure 5.4 Wiener Model

For the present simulation results $G_L(z)$ and $f(v)$ were chosen as

$$G_L(z) = \frac{0.0187z^{-1} + 0.0175z^{-2}}{1 - 1.64z^{-1} + 0.6929z^{-2}} \tag{5.50}$$

$$y(k) = f(v(k)) = \arctan(v(k)). \tag{5.51}$$

The structure of Wiener systems enables a simple representation of nonlinear systems. The nonlinearity $f(v)$ has full impact on the output and stability analysis can become challenging, in particular when the nonlinearity has a saturation character like in the present example, [1, 55].

In this example the input $u(k)$ is bounded to the interval $[-3, 3]$.

An LMN comprising six local models was generated by the algorithm presented in [22], where the local models are constructed using an axis oblique decomposition of the partition space. Figure 5.5 shows the identification data as well as a contour plot of the validity functions where its input vector is as follows:

$$\tilde{x}(k) = [u(k-1)\ \hat{y}(k-1)]. \tag{5.52}$$

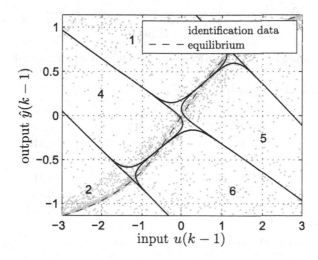

Figure 5.5 Contour plot of the validity functions and identification data sequence

Figure 5.6 illustrates the outputs of the Wiener model $y(k)$ and the LMN $\hat{y}(k)$ for the same input sequence $u(k)$. Thus, the good approximation capability of the LMN is illustrated.

In order to demonstrate the effectiveness of the proposed method two different PID controllers are compared. Controller A is the conventional controller where the controller parameters are locally determined by using auto-PID command from the Toolbox of MATLAB®. The parameters of controller A are used as initial set for the iLMI procedure. Controller B is the guaranteed stable controller. The parameters which were determined by means of the iLMI method presented in Section 5.4.1.

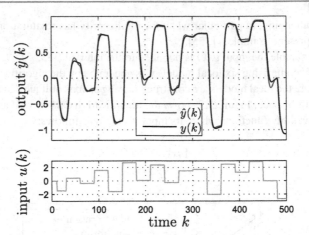

Figure 5.6 Comparison of the open loop behavior of the process and the LMN

Table 5.1 Parameters of controller A

Model #	K_p	T_N	T_V
1	9.481	79.817	1.039
2	5.778	4.043	0.649
3	5.519	4.029	0.649
4	2.878	7.418	0.722
5	2.934	7.603	0.726
6	9.240	79.762	0.986

Table 5.2 Parameters of controller B

Model #	K_p	T_N	T_V
1	0.664	4.538	1.908
2	0.073	1.638	18.588
3	0.092	2.046	14.834
4	0.830	4.973	1.947
5	0.821	4.883	1.947
6	0.637	4.393	2.011

The parameters sets of the two controllers are given in Table 5.1 and Table 5.2, respectively.

In Figure 5.7(a) the oscillatory behavior using controller A shows a poor controller performance and the strongly different damping indicates that a stability proof will be difficult. Nevertheless, the closed loop with controller A may be stable although a stability proof fails because Lyapunov stability criteria are sufficient rather than necessary conditions. The closed loop stability of the LMN controlled by controller B is guaranteed because of the usage of Theorem 5.1. The controller performance in the time domain looks good as well, see Figure 5.7(a). The closed loop performance also depends on the approximation capability of the LMN. This becomes visible when the local controller network is applied to the actual plant rather than to the LMN, see Figure 5.7(b).

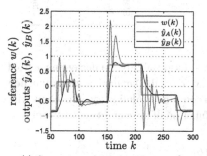 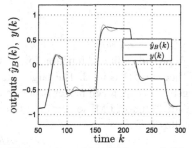

(a) Comparison of the closed loop performance of the LMN with two PID controllers
Controller A: initial design; no stability assertion possible
Controller B: iLMI stabilized; exponentially stable, $\alpha = 0.98$

(b) Comparison of the LMN output $\hat{y}_B(k)$ and the output of the original process $y(k)$ controlled by the globally stable controller

Figure 5.7 Comparison plots of the PID controlled LMN

5.4.2 Multi-Objective GA

In this section a methodology is introduced which handles the trade-off between *stability* and *performance* of the closed loop. For this purpose, a multiGA [91] is used. The basic concept is depicted in Figure 5.8. Due to the fact that the proposed PID controller design method aims to yield satisfactory controller performance as well as guaranteed closed loop stability both fitness criteria are considered by the proposed method:

Figure 5.8 Scheme of the
combination of genetic
algorithm with stability and
performance criteria

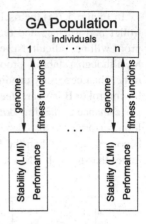

- *Stability Criterion*
  To provide a fitness function for the closed loop stability the decay rate α from Theorem 5.1 is used. The larger the decay rate, the larger the fitness function gets. This approach makes it possible to combine evolutionary algorithms with state of the art LMI solvers. The fitness function of the stability assessment is as follows:
  $$f_S = \alpha(K_{PID}^{(i)}, \forall i \in \mathcal{I}) \tag{5.53}$$

- *Performance Criterion*
  To quantify the closed loop controller performance, a proper reference signal is generated with design of experiments (DoE) methods. The fitness function of the performance is based on a permission window. When the system output leaves this window the fitness function is increased. The performance criterion is explained in Section 5.4.2.1.

Remark 5.6 *The introduced concept is not limited to Genetic Algorithms. Other evolutionary algorithms such as multi-objective particle swarm pptimization (multiPSO, [96, 97]) may also be used.*

The Genetic Algorithm uses a direct analogy to natural evolution, where stronger individuals are likely to be the winner in a competitive environment, [83].

The GA uses a parameter set, usually called genome, that represents an individual and may be a potential solution of a problem. A positive value, commonly known as fitness function, is used to represent the "strength" of a genome. Due to a genetic evolution the fitter genome tends to yield good quality offsprings, which evolves a better solution of the problem. In each cycle of the GA (evolution) a group of genomes (parents) or a collection pool are selected via a specific fitness accordant selection routine. The genes of the parents are mixed and recombined for offspring in the next generation. It is expected that the "stronger" genome will create a larger number of offsprings and thus a higher chance of surviving the subsequent generation.

Further, mutations of the offsprings are used in GAs. A large mutation rate increases diversity of the algorithm but tends to distract the algorithm from converging to an optimum, [98].

The main advantage of *multi-objective* GAs to conventional (single-objective) optimization methods is the ability to get multiple trade-off solutions where no solution of the set of these optimal solutions can be said to be better than the other, [91]. Such a set of optimal solutions is commonly called the pareto-optimal front, see Figure 5.9.

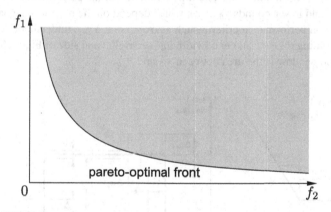

Figure 5.9 Exemplary pareto-optimal front

In the following a multi objective optimization problem is stated in its general form, [91]:

$$\begin{aligned}
\text{min/max} \quad & f_m(x_{opt}), \quad && m = 1, \ldots, M \\
\text{subject to} \quad & g_j(x_{opt}) \geq 0, \quad && j = 1, \ldots, J \\
& h_k(x_{opt}) = 0, \quad && k = 1, \ldots, K \\
& x_i^{(lb)} \leq x_i \leq x_i^{(ub)}, \quad && i = 1, \ldots, n
\end{aligned} \tag{5.54}$$

A solution x_{opt} is a vector of n decision variables: $x_{opt} = (x_1, x_2, \ldots, x_n)^T$. The last set of constraints is called variable bounds, restricting each decision variable

x_i to take a value within a range from $x_i^{(lb)}$ to $x_i^{(ub)}$. These bounds constitute the decision space $\mathcal{D}$.

Detailed information on genetic algorithms can be found in e.g. [23, 91, 92, 99].

According to the PID control algorithm for LMNs the genome contains all PID controller parameters:

$$\mathcal{G} = \left\{ d_{p.0}^{(i)}, d_{p.1}^{(i)}, d_{p.2}^{(i)} \right\}, \ \forall p \in \mathcal{P}, \ \forall i \in \mathcal{I} \qquad (5.55)$$

5.4.2.1 Performance Criterion

As basis for the performance criterion a reference signal $w_p(k)$ is generated which results from a suitable Design of Experiments, [56]. This signal covers the whole output space of the LMN to capture the global nonlinear closed loop performance and its length is denoted as K. The fitness function of the performance f_p is based on upper- and lower bounds y_{ub}, y_{lb} which depend on the reference signal $w_p(k)$ and common performance criteria such as overshoot Δy_{os}, undershoot Δy_{us}, rise time k_r, settling time k_s, and bandwidth bw, see right hand side of Figure 5.10. The permission window is the area between y_{lb} and y_{ub}.

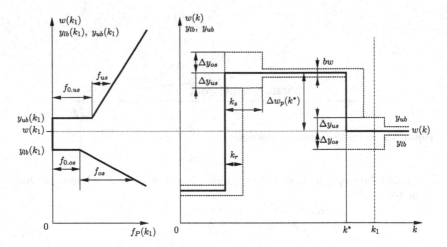

Figure 5.10 Fitness function and performance window of the Performance Criterion

The fitness function for the closed loop performance follows from Figure 5.10. Accordingly

$$f_P = \sum_{k \in \{\mathbb{N}|1,\dots,K\}} f_P(k) \tag{5.56}$$

$$f_P(k) = \begin{cases} f_{0.os} + f_{os} & \text{sign}(\Delta w_p(k^*))(y(k) - y_{ub}(k)) > 0 \\ 0 & y_{lb} \le y(k) \le y_{ub}(k) \\ f_{0.us} + f_{us} & \text{sign}(\Delta w_p(k^*))(y(k) - y_{lb}(k)) < 0 \end{cases} \tag{5.57}$$

with

$$f_{os} = \begin{cases} c_{os}|y(k) - y_{ub}(k)| & \text{sign}(\Delta w_p(k^*)) = 1 \\ c_{os}|y(k) - y_{lb}(k)| & \text{sign}(\Delta w_p(k^*)) = -1 \end{cases}$$

$$f_{us} = \begin{cases} c_{us}|y(k) - y_{ub}(k)| & \text{sign}(\Delta w_p(k^*)) = -1 \\ c_{us}|y(k) - y_{lb}(k)| & \text{sign}(\Delta w_p(k^*)) = 1 \end{cases}$$

where c_{os} and c_{us} are coefficients for the growth of the fitness function when the system output $\hat{y}(k)$ leaves the permitted area, see Figure 5.10.

5.4.2.2 Example: Dynamic Nonlinear Process

For illustrative purposes, a nonlinear dynamic process is considered. The basic concept of this process is taken from [10, 61] and and extended to a MISO system. It can be described by the following difference equation:

$$\begin{aligned} y(k) =& 0.07u_1(k-1) - 0.04u_1(k-2) + 0.09u_2(k-1) - 0.05u_2(k-2) + 0.6y(k-1) \\ & - 0.5y(k-2) + (u_1(k-1) + u_2(k-2))[0.08y(k-1) - 0.09y(k-2)] \end{aligned} \tag{5.58}$$

In this example the input $u(k)$ is bounded to the interval $[-1.5\ 0.5]$.

For system identification an excitation signal was generated to capture both the nonlinear dynamic and static behavior, [56].

From these data, an LMN comprising five local models was generated by the algorithm presented in [22], where the local models are defined by an axis oblique decomposition of the partition space. The partition space is defined as

$$\tilde{x} = \begin{bmatrix} u_1(k-1) & u_2(k-1) & \hat{y}(k-1) \end{bmatrix} \tag{5.59}$$

The partitioning strategy in [22] uses statistical methods to avoid overfitting by local models generated with only few observations. The input orders and the output order were set equally to the orders of the plant:

$$m_1 = \{1, 2\}, \ m_2 = \{1, 2\}, \ n = \{1, 2\} \tag{5.60}$$

Figure 5.11 demonstrates the excellent approximation quality of the identified LMN:

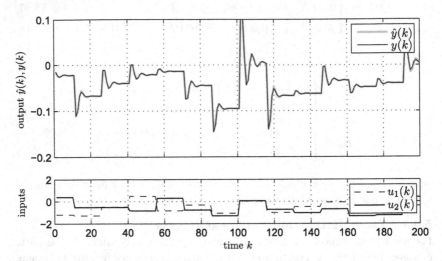

Figure 5.11 Comparison of the open loop behavior of the process and the LMN by means of a cross-validation

Input 2 was selected as control input:

$$\mathcal{P} = 2, \ \mathcal{R} = 1 \tag{5.61}$$

Figure 5.12 demonstrates the performance of a PID controller network where the local PID parameters were determined by the MATLAB® command pidtune. This algorithm is based on [69] and automatically tunes the PID gains to balance performance (response time) and robustness (stability margins), [100]. The algorithm chooses a crossover frequency (loop bandwidth) based upon the plant dynamics, and designs for a target phase margin of 60°. This controller shows a poor performance. Nevertheless, the closed loop is stable with a decay rate of $\alpha = 0.9935$.

Figure 5.13 shows the closed loop performance of a PID controller network designed by the proposed method. The GA achieves the following fitness functions:

$$\alpha = f_S = 0.8360, \ f_P = 3.4552 \tag{5.62}$$

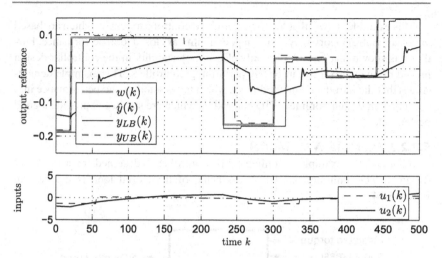

Figure 5.12 Closed loop performance of a locally tuned based PID controller

It is shown that this controller achieves both a good performance and a low decay rate. Furthermore, the disturbance rejection is also quite good.

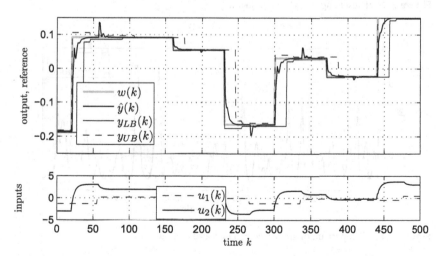

Figure 5.13 Closed loop performance of the GA based PID controller

This example shows, that locally determined control parameters which are based on linear control theory may result in poor nonlinear closed loop performance. Further it is shown that considering only closed loop stability in the controller design procedure may also result in poorly performing controllers. This example demonstrates that the introduced methodology, which takes stability and performance into account, can design nonlinear PID controllers which are stable and provide a good performance.

5.4.2.3 Example: NO_x Model

In the presented example a nonlinear PID controller is designed for a nonlinear dynamic NO_x emission model. The scheme of the closed loop is depicted in Figure 5.14.

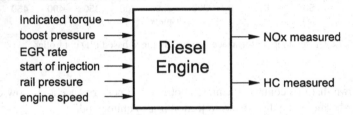

Figure 5.14 Diesel engine exhaust modelling

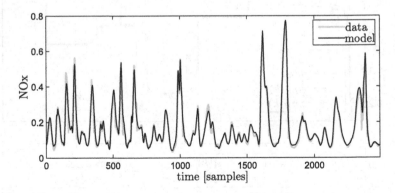

Figure 5.15 Comparison of simulated and measured output

An LMN obtained from measurement data, [101], is used as engine model to get reproducible results. As control input the start of injection (SOI) is used while all other inputs (indicated torque, boost pressure, EGR (exhaust gas recirculation) rate, rail pressure, engine speed) are considered. As reference signal $NO_{x,dmd}$ the NO_x signal from the training data record is reduced to 85%. All inputs and the output are used to define the partition space. Thus, the validity function depends on all inputs and the output. Both in- and output data are scaled between 0 and 1.

In Fig. 5.15 a comparison of simulated and measured output (NOx) is presented. The LMN accurately describes the true process at the generalization data record and a normalized root mean square error of 2.68% was obtained using the proposed LMN. In the presented example a nonlinear PID controller is designed by means of an LMN which approximates NO_x. The scheme of the closed loop is depicted in Figure 5.16.

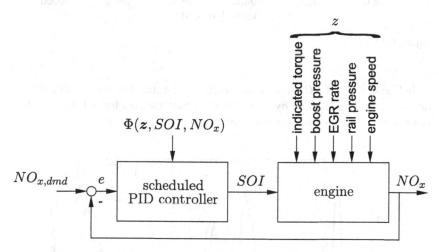

Figure 5.16 Control scheme

The LMN is used as engine model to get reproducible results. As manipulating variable the start of injection (SOI) is used. All other inputs (indicated torque, boost pressure, EGR rate, rail pressure, engine speed) are modelled as disturbances. As reference signal $NO_{x,dmd}$ the NO_x signal from the training data is reduced to 85%. All inputs and the output are used to define the partition space. Thus, the validity function depends on all inputs and the output.

Figure 5.17 shows the NO_x signals from the identification data and the output of the simulated closed loop. A significant reduction of the NO_x peaks is achieved by using the nonlinear PID controller.

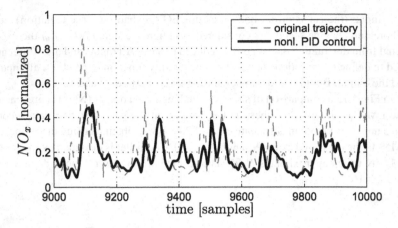

Figure 5.17 NO_x

In Figure 5.18 the SOI, torque and speed are depicted. The significant peaks of the SOI signal are induced by the fact that the presented nonlinear PID controller is not limited to a specific operating area.

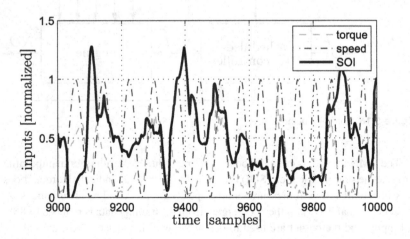

Figure 5.18 System Inputs

Figure 5.19 shows the cumulated NO_x from the identification data and the simulation result. It is visible that the desired NO_x reduction to 85% of the original value is achieved.

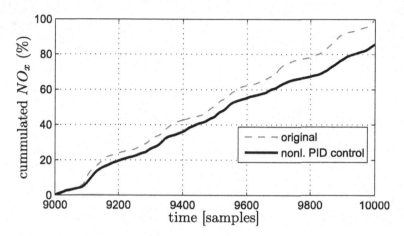

Figure 5.19 Cumulated NO_x

The shown controller design achieves a decay rate of $\alpha = 1.001$, where no stability assertion is possible. Nevertheless, the result of Figure 5.17 indicates a globally stable closed loop although the proof is not possible.

Conclusion and Outlook

6

The motivation for this work was the increasing usage of model based methods in automotive applications. Especially in controller calibration of internal combustion engines there is a high potential to reduce development cost by reducing measurement time on engine testbeds. For the usage of LMNs in automotive engineering it is vital to provide stability criteria of the models. Furthermore, methods for controller calibration have been developed to provide an effective workflow for controller calibration in automotive engineering.

In the first part of this work a method for the quantitative comparison of different Lyapunov approaches for complex discrete-time LMNs has been proposed. For this purpose three basic Lyapunov approaches were extended by the decay rate which provides a measure for the conservatism. The concept of using the decay rate to compare the conservatism can be easily used for most of the existing approaches and is an interesting alternative to existing methods. Secondly, a method was introduced which determines the model transitions by means of the identification data sequence. This transition determination method significantly reduces the conservatism of the piecewise quadratic and the fuzzy Lyapunov approach. Simulation examples have been used to illustrate the conservatism of different Lyapunov approaches and the influence of the transition determination method.

The second part investigates closed loop stability and controller design methods for LMNs. The focus of the controller design methods was on state-feedback and PID controllers which are based on a LMN. The design method of PID controller includes a Lyapunov stability criterion to guarantee stable closed loop performance. For the sake of simplicity only multiGA, a basic common quadratic Lyapunov criterion and a simple performance criterion is used. The computational cost is significantly higher than for common state-feedback controller design but could be kept acceptable because of the relatively simple stability criterion. A good convergence behavior was demonstrated by means of an example. The main limitation of

C. Mayr, *Stability Analysis and Controller Design of Local Model Networks*, https://doi.org/10.1007/978-3-658-34008-7_6

the proposed method is the limited calculation power of the used computer. However, evolutionary algorithms are suitable for computer-clusters which may solve this issue. In further work, other multi-objective optimization methods (e.g.: multi-objective particle swarm optimization), more advanced stability criteria (e.g.: fuzzy Lyapunov approach) and other performance criteria may be investigated.

Future developments are focused on the adaption to and integration into specific ECU architectures and controllers for automotive application. Further, advance controller design methods will be investigated, such as fuzzy model predictive control (fuzzy MPC) and robust controller design methods ($\mathcal{H}_\infty$). A good overview of various controller design methods and possible reductions of the conservatism of Lyapunov approaches is given in [43].

LMI Solver Comparison

Introduction

This chapter treats the performance of various LMI solvers. There are many free and commercial LMI solvers available. The numerical performance of LMI solvers is vital especially for solving BMIs by means of a genetic algorithm and an LMI solver. In Table A.1 the reviewed solvers are given.

Table A.1 Reviewed LMI solvers

Solver	Kind	Source
gevp	commercial	MATLAB® Robust Control Toolbox, [47]
feas	commercial	MATLAB® Robust Control Toolbox, [47]
mincx	commercial	MATLAB® Robust Control Toolbox, [47]
SeDuMi	free	SeDuMi Homepage[1], [48]
Sdpt3	free	Sdpt3 Homepage[2], [49]
CVX	free/commercial	CVX Homepage[3], [107]

The toolbox YALMIP can be strongly recommended as modeling language for advanced modeling and solution of convex and nonconvex optimization problems. It is free and supports a large number of optimization classes, such as linear, quadratic, second order cone, semidefinite, mixed integer conic, geometric, local and global

---

[1] http://sedumi.ie.lehigh.edu
[2] http://www.math.nus.edu.sg/~mattohkc/sdpt3.html
[3] http://cvxr.com/cvx/

© The Editor(s) (if applicable) and The Author(s), under exclusive license to Springer Fachmedien Wiesbaden GmbH, part of Springer Nature 2021
C. Mayr, *Stability Analysis and Controller Design of Local Model Networks*,
https://doi.org/10.1007/978-3-658-34008-7

polynomial, multiparametric, bilevel and robust programming. One of the central ideas in YALMIP is to concentrate on the language and the higher level algorithms, while relying on external solvers for the actual computations, [108, 109].

Comparison

The calculation effort of the LMI solvers was compared by means of a Wiener Model. Figure A.1 depicts the calculation times for the reviewed LMI solvers by means of the common quadratic Lyapunov approach.

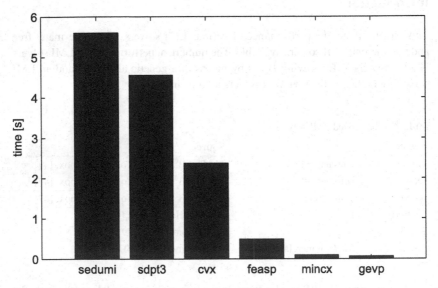

Figure A.1 Calculation time for the reviewed LMI solvers

The results of Figure A.1 show that the solvers from the MATLAB® Robust Control Toolbox need the smallest calculation time. It is assumed that the reason is that these solvers are especially programmed for solving LMIs. The other solvers are more versatile and thus not so efficient in solving LMIs. Thus, the gevp solver should be used whenever it is possible. As mentioned in Chapter 3 another advantage of the gevp solver is the inherent implementation of the decay rate which allows exponential stability analysis for LMNs on the one hand and a quantitative comparison of various stability approaches on the other hand. However, the solvers

Table A.2 Advantages and disadvantages of the reviewed LMI solver

Robust Control Toolbox	SeDuMi/Sdpt3/CVX
+ Numerically robust	+ Versatile
+ Calculation effort	+ Simple syntax
− Complex syntax	+ Standard interfaces available (Yalmip)
− Only for symmetric problems	− Calculation effort
− No equality constraints	− Numerically less robust

SeDuMi, Sdpt3 and CVX allow the investigation of equality constraints which is not possible for the LMI solvers of the MATLAB® Robust Control Toolbox. A short review of the advantages and disadvantages of the different approaches is given in Table A.2.

References

1. S. Jakubek, C. Hametner, and K. N, "Total Least Squares in Fuzzy System Identification," *Engineering Applications of Artificial Intelligence*, pp. 1277–1288, 2008.
2. C. Hametner, "Nonlinear Dynamic System Identification Using Local Model Architectures," *thesis*, pp. 1–118, Nov. 2007.
3. C. Hametner and M. Nebel, "Operating regime based dynamic engine modelling," *Control Engineering Practice*, vol. 20, no. 4, pp. 397–407, Apr. 2012.
4. J.-J. E. Slotine and W. Li, *Applied Nonlinear Control*, 1991.
5. S. Jakubek, "Proposal for Founding and Funding of the Christian Doppler Laboratory for Model based calibration methodologies," pp. 1–71, 2009.
6. R. Gao, *Local Model Network Application in Control*, 2004.
7. G. Gregorcic and G. Lightbody, "Local Model Network Identification With Gaussian Processes," *IEEE Transactions on Neural Networks*, vol. 18, no. 5, pp. 1404–1423, Sept. 2007.
8. J. Novak and V. Bobal, "Predictive Control of the Heat Exchanger using Local Model Network," in *Proceedings of the 17th Mediterranean Conference on Control & Automation*, June 2009, pp. 657–662.
9. S. Jakubek and C. Hametner, "Identification of Neurofuzzy Models Using GTLS Parameter Estimation," *IEEE Transactions on Systems, Man, and Cybernetics, Part B: Cybernetics*, vol. 39, no. 5, pp. 1121–1133, Oct. 2009.
10. O. Nelles, *Nonlinear System Identification: From Classical Approaches to Neural Networks and Fuzzy Models*. Springer Verlag London Berlin Heidelberg, 2001.
11. I. Skrjanc and S. Blazic, "Identification of dynamical systems with a robust interval fuzzy model," *Automatica*, vol. 41, pp. 327–332, 2005.
12. B. Hartmann, O. Banfer, O. Nelles, A. Sodja, L. Teslic, and I. Skrjanc, "Supervised Hierarchical Clustering in Fuzzy Model Identification," *IEEE Transactions on Fuzzy Systems*, vol. 19, no. 6, pp. 1163–1176, 2011.
13. L. Teslic, B. Hartmann, O. Nelles, and I. Skrjanc, "Nonlinear System Identification by Gustafson-Kessel Fuzzy Clustering and Supervised Local Model Network Learning for the Drug Absorption Spectra Process," *IEEE Transactions on Neural Networks*, vol. 22, no. 12, pp. 1941–1951, 2011.

14. T. Takagi and M. Sugeno, "Fuzzy Identification of Systems and its Applications to Modeling and Control," *IEEE Transactions on Systems, Man, and Cybernetics*, vol. 15, no. 1, pp. 116–132, 1985.

15. G. Gregorcic and G. Lightbody, "Nonlinear System Identification: From Multiple-Model Networks to Gaussian Processes," *Engineering Applications of Artificial Intelligence*, vol. 21, no. 7, pp. 1035–1055, 2008.

16. J. Park and I. W. Sandberg, "Universal Approximation Using Radial-Basis-Function Networks," *Neural Computation*, vol. 3, no. 2, pp. 246–257, 1991.

17. C. Hametner and S. Jakubek, "New Concepts for the Identification of Dynamic Takagi-Sugeno Fuzzy Models," in *IEEE Conference on Cybernetics and Intelligent Systems*, June 2006, pp. 185–190.

18. K. Tanaka and M. Sugeno, "Stability Analysis and Design of Fuzzy Control Systems," *Fuzzy Sets and Systems*, vol. 45, no. 2, pp. 135–156, 1992.

19. O. Nelles, "Local Linear Model Trees for On-Line Identification of Time-Variant Nonlinear Dynamic Systems," *International Conference on Artificial Neural Networks*, 1996.

20. L. Thanh Ngo, L. Pham The, P. Hoang Nguyen, and K. Hirota, *On Approximate Representation of Type-2 Fuzzy Sets Using Triangulated Irregular Networ*, P. Melin, O. Castillo, L. T. Aguilar, J. Kacprzyk, and W. Pedrycz, Eds. Berlin, Heidelberg: Foundations of Fuzzy Logic and Soft Computiong, 2007, vol. 4529.

21. S. Jakubek and N. Keuth, "A Local Neuro-Fuzzy Network for High-Dimensional Models and Optimization," *Engineering Applications of Artificial Intelligence*, vol. 19, pp. 705–717, 2006.

22. C. Hametner and S. Jakubek, "Neuro-Fuzzy Modelling Using a Logistic Discriminant Tree," in *Proceedings of the 2007 American Control Conference*, July 2007, pp. 864–869.

23. J. Causa, G. Karer, A. Núñez, D. Sáez, I. Skrjanc, and B. Zupancic, "Hybrid fuzzy predictive control based on genetic algorithms for the temperature control of a batch reactor," *Computers & Chemical Engineering*, vol. 32, no. 12, pp. 254–3263, Dec. 2008.

24. L. Breiman, "Classification and regression trees," 1984.

25. P. Pucar and M. Millnert, "Smooth hinging hyperplanes-an alternative to neural nets," in *Proceedings of 3rd European Control Conference*, 1995.

26. S. Ernst, "Hinging hyperplane trees for approximation and identification," in *Proceedings of the 37th IEEE Conference on Decision and Control*, 1998, pp. 1266–1271.

27. C. M. Bishop, *Neural networks for pattern recognition*. Oxford University Press, USA, 1995.

28. A. Lyapunov, "The General Problem of the Stability of Motion," *International Journal of Control*, vol. 55, no. 3, pp. 531–773, 1992.

29. G. Feng, "A Survey on Analysis and Design of Model-based Fuzzy Control Systems," *IEEE Transactions on Fuzzy Systems*, vol. 14, no. 5, pp. 676–697, 2006.

30. G. Feng, "Stability Analysis of Discrete-Time Fuzzy Dynamic Systems Based on Piecewise Lyapunov Functions," *IEEE Transactions on Fuzzy Systems*, vol. 12, no. 1, pp. 22–28, 2004.

31. G. Feng, *Analysis and Synthesis of Fuzzy Control Systems*, ser. A Model Based Approach. Boca Raton: CRC Press, Taylor & Francis Group, Feb. 2010.

32. M. Johansson and A. Rantzer, "Computation of Piecewise Quadratic Lyapunov Functions for Hybrid Systems," *IEEE Transactions on Automatic Control*, vol. 43, no. 4, pp. 555–559, 1998.

33. M. Johansson and A. Rantzer, "Piecewise Quadratic Stability of Fuzzy Systems," *IEEE Transactions on Fuzzy Systems*, vol. 7, no. 6, pp. 713–722, 2000.

34. Y. Wang, Z. Sun, and F. Sun, "Stability Analysis and Control of Discrete-time Fuzzy Systems: A Fuzzy Lyapunov Function Approach," *Proceedings of the 5th Asian Control Conference*, 2004.

35. C. Sun, Y. Su, and C. Chuang, "Relaxed Stabilization Criterion for TS Fuzzy Discrete System," 2009.

36. E. Kim and H. Lee, "New Approaches to Relaxed Quadratic Stability Condition of Fuzzy Control Systems," *IEEE Transactions on Fuzzy Systems*, vol. 8, no. 5, pp. 523–534, 2000.

37. E. Kim and D. Kim, "Stability Analysis and Synthesis for an Affine Fuzzy System via LMI and ILMI: Discrete Case," *IEEE Transactions on Systems, Man, and Cybernetics, Part B: Cybernetics*, vol. 31, no. 1, pp. 132–140, 2001.

38. T. M. Guerra, A. Kruszewski, and M. Bernal, "Control Law Proposition for the Stabilization of Discrete Takagi-Sugeno Models," *IEEE Transactions on Fuzzy Systems*, vol. 17, no. 3, pp. 724–731, 2009.

39. T. Guerra and L. Vermeiren, "LMI-based relaxed nonquadratic stabilization conditions for nonlinear systems in the Takagi-Sugeno's form", *Automatica*, 2004.

40. B. Ding, H. Sun, and P. Yang, "Further studies on LMI-based relaxed stabilization conditions for nonlinear systems in Takgi-Sugeno's form", *Automatica*, 2006.

41. A. Kruszewski, R. Wang, and T. M. Guerra, "Nonquadratic Stabilization Conditions for a Class of Uncertain Nonlinear Discrete Time TS Fuzzy Models: A New Approach," *IEEE Transactions on Automatic Control*, vol. 53, no. 2, pp. 606–611, 2008.

42. S. Zhou, J. Lam, and A. Xue, "$H_{-\infty}$ filtering of discrete-time fuzzy systems via basis-dependent Lyapunov function approach," *Fuzzy Sets and Systems*, vol. 158, no. 2, pp. 180–193, 2007.

43. H.-K. Lam and F. H.-F. Leung, *Stability Analysis of Fuzzy-Model-Based Control Systems*. Springer-Verlag New York Inc, Jan. 2011.

44. C. Mayr, C. Hametner, M. Kozek, and S. Jakubek, "Relaxed Fuzzy Lyapunov Approach for Dynamic Local Model Networks," in *Proceedings of the 2011 IEEE International Conference on Fuzzy Systems*. Christian Doppler Laboratory for Model Based Calibration Methodologies, Vienna University of Technology, 2011.

45. M. Bernal and P. Husek, "Non-Quadratic Performance Design for Takagi-Sugeno Fuzzy Systems," *International Journal of Applied Mathematics and Computer Science*, vol. 15, no. 3, pp. 383–391, 2005.

46. K. Tanaka and H. O Wang, "Fuzzy Control Systems Design and Analysis: a Linear Matrix Inequality Approach," *John Wiley & Sons, Inc.*, p. 305, 2001.

47. Y. Nesterov and A. Nemirovskii, *Interior-Point Polynomial Algorithms in Convex Programming*, siam ed., ser. Theory and Application. Philadelphia: Society for Industrial Mathematics, Jan. 1994.

48. J. Sturm, "Using SeDuMi 1. 02, a MATLAB toolbox for optimization over symmetric cones," *Optimization Methods and Software*, vol. 11-12, no. Special issue on Interior Point Methods, pp. 625–653, 1999.

49. K. Toh and M. Todd, "SDPT 3 – A MATLAB Software Package for Semidefinite Programming," *Optimization Methods and Software*, vol. 11, pp. 545–581, Sept. 1999.

50. C. Mayr, C. Hametner, M. Kozek, and S. Jakubek, "Piecewise Quadratic Stability Analysis for Local Model Networks," in *Proceedings of the 2011 IEEE Multi-conference on System and Control*. Christian Doppler Laboratory for Model Based Calibration Methodologies, Vienna University of Technology, 2011.

51. S. Cao, N. Rees, and G. Feng, "Quadratic Stability Analysis and Design of Continuous-Time Fuzzy Control Systems," *International Journal of Systems Science*, vol. 27, no. 2, pp. 193–203, 1996.

52. S. Cao, "Analysis and Design for a Class of Complex Control Systems Part II: Fuzzy Controller Design," *Automatica*, vol. 33, no. 6, pp. 1029–1039, 1997.

53. S. Cao, N. Rees, and G. Feng, "Stability Analysis and Design for a Class of Continuous-Time Fuzzy Control Systems," *International Journal of Control*, vol. 64, no. 6, pp. 1069–1087, 1996.

54. I. Skrjanc, S. Blazic, O. E. S. M. Agamennoni, and C. P. B. C. I. T. on, "Interval fuzzy modeling applied to Wiener models with uncertainties," *IEEE Transactions on Systems, Man, and Cybernetics, Part B: Cybernetics*, vol. 35, no. 5.

55. M. Kozek and N. Jovanovic, "Identification of Hammerstein/Wiener nonlinear systems with extended Kalman filters," *Proceedings of the American control conference*, vol. 2, pp. 969–962, May 2002.

56. G. C. Goodwin and R. L Payne, "Dynamic System Identification: Experiment Design and Data Analysis," *Mathematics in Science and Engineering*, vol. 136, p. 291, 1977.

57. K. Tanaka, T. Hori, and H. Wang, "A Multiple Lyapunov Function Approach to Stabilization of Fuzzy Control Systems," *IEEE Transactions on Fuzzy Systems*, vol. 11, no. 4, pp. 582–589, 2003.

58. S. Zhou, G. Feng, J. Lam, and S. Xu, "Robust H_∞ Control for Discrete-time Fuzzy Systems via Basis-dependent Lyapunov Functions," *Information Sciences*, vol. 174, pp. 197–217, 2005.

59. S. Zhou, J. Lam, and W. X. Zheng, "Control Design for Fuzzy Systems Based on Relaxed Nonquadratic Stability and H Performance Conditions," *IEEE Transactions on Fuzzy Systems*, vol. 15, no. 2, pp. 188–199, 2007.

60. H.-N. Wu, "Delay-Dependent Stability Analysis and Stabilization for Discrete-Time Fuzzy Systems With State Delay: A Fuzzy Lyapunov-Krasovskii Functional Approach," *IEEE Transactions on Systems, Man, and Cybernetics, Part B: Cybernetics*, vol. 36, no. 4, pp. 954–962, 2006.

61. I. Leontaritis and S. Billings, "Input-Output Parametric Models for Non-linear Systems Part I: Deterministic Non-linear Systems," *International Journal of Control*, vol. 41, no. 2, pp. 303–328, 1985.

62. K. J. Hunt and T. A. Johansen, "Design and analysis of gain-scheduled control using local controller networks," *International Journal of Control*, vol. 66, no. 5, pp. 619–651, 1997.

63. A. Fink, S. Toepfer, and R. Isermann, "Nonlinear Model-Based Control with Local Linear Neuro-Fuzzy Models," *Archive of Applied Mechanics (Ingenieur Archiv)*, pp. 911–922, June 2003.

64. K. Kiriakidis, "Non-linear control system design via fuzzy modelling and LMIs," *International Journal of Control*, vol. 72, no. 7, pp. 676–685, Dec. 1998.

65. I. Skrjanc and S. Blazic, "Predictive Functional Control Based on Fuzzy Model: Design and Stability Study." *Journal of Intelligent and Robotic Systems*, vol. 43, pp. 283–299, 2005.

66. T. Guerra, A. Kruszewski, and L. Vermeiren, "Conditions of output stabilization for nonlinear models in the Takagi-Sugeno's form", *Fuzzy Sets and Systems*, vol. 157, no. 9, pp. 1248–1259, 2006.

67. S. Blazic and I. Skrjanc, "Design and Stability Analysis of Fuzzy Model-based Predictive Control – A Case Study." *Journal of Intelligent and Robotic Systems*, vol. 49, no. 3, pp. 279–292, 2007.

68. M. Bernal, T. Guerra, and A. Kruszewski, "A membership-function-dependent approach for stability analysis and controller synthesis of Takagi-Sugeno models," *Fuzzy Sets and Systems*, vol. 160, no. 19, pp. 2776–2795, 2009.

69. K. J. Åström and T. Hägglund, *Advanced PID control*. ISA – The Instrumentation, Systems, and Automation Society, Research Triangle Park, NC 27709, 2006.

70. A. Leva, "PID Autotuning Algorithm-Based on Relay Feedback," *IEEE Proceedings-D Control Theory and Applications*, vol. 140, no. 5, pp. 328–338, 1993.

71. R. Sanchis, J. A. Romero, and P. Balaguer, "Tuning of PID controllers based on simplified single parameter optimisation," *International Journal of Control*, vol. 83, no. 9, pp. 1785–1798, 2010.

72. J. Kocijan, D. Vrancic, G. Dolanc, S. Gerksic, S. Strmcnik, I. Skrjanc, S. Blazic, M. Bozicek, Z. Marinsek, M. Hadjiski, K. Boshnakov, A. Stathaki, and R. King, "Auto-tuning non-linear controller for industrial use," in *IEEE International Conference on Industrial Technology*, 2003, pp. 906–911.

73. M.-D. Hua and C. Samson, "Time sub-optimal nonlinear PI and PID controllers applied to longitudinal headway car control," *International Journal of Control*, vol. 84, no. 10, pp. 1717–1728, 2011.

74. H. Gollee and K. J. Hunt, "Nonlinear modelling and control of electrically stimulated muscle: A local model network approach," *International Journal of Control*, vol. 68, no. 6, pp. 1259–1288, Jan. 1997.

75. M. Nebel, M.-S. Vogels, T. Combe, T. Winsel, H. Pfluegl, and C. Hametner, "Global Dynamic Models for XiL-based Calibration," Warrendale, PA, Tech. Rep., Apr. 2010.

76. C. Hametner, J. Edelmann, S. Jakubek, and W. Mack, "An advanced algorithm for partitioning and parameter estimation in local model networks and its application to vehicle vertical dynamics," *Acta Mechanica*, pp. 1–14, 2012.

77. C. Hametner and S. Jakubek, "Local model network identification for online engine modelling," *Information Sciences*, vol. 220, pp. 210–225, 2012.

78. G. Chen and H. Ying, "BIBO Stability of Nonlinear Fuzzy PI Control Systems," *Journal of Intelligent Fuzzy Systems*, vol. 5, pp. 245–256, 1997.

79. Y. Ding, H. Ying, and S. Shao, "Typical Takagi-Sugeno PI and PD fuzzy controllers: analytical structures and stability analysis," *Information Sciences*, vol. 151, pp. 245–262, 2003.

80. G. Mann and R. Gosine, "New methodology for analytical and optimal design of fuzzy PID controllers," *IEEE Transactions on Fuzzy Systems*, vol. 7, no. 5, pp. 521–539, 1999.

81. B. Mohan and A. Sinha, "Analytical structure and stability analysis of a fuzzy PID controller," *Applied Soft Computing*, vol. 8, pp. 749–758, 2008.

82. K. Sio and C. Lee, "Stability of fuzzy PID controllers," *IEEE Transactions on Systems, Man, and Cybernetics-Part A: Systems and Humans*, vol. 28, no. 4, pp. 490–495, 1998.

83. K. Tang, K. F. Man, G. Chen, and S. Kwong, "An optimal fuzzy PID controller," *IEEE Transactions on Industrial Electronics*, vol. 48, no. 4, pp. 757–765, 2001.

84. J. Carvajal and G. Chen, "Fuzzy PID controller: Design, performance evaluation, and stability analysis," *Information Sciences*, vol. 123, no. 3–4, pp. 249–270, 2000.

85. T. Guerra and A. Kruszewski, "Discrete Tagaki-Sugeno models for control: Where are we?" *Annual Reviews in Control*, vol. 33, no. 1, pp. 37–47, 2009.

86. C. Mayr, C. Hametner, M. Kozek, and S. Jakubek, "Nonlinear Stable PID Controller Design using Local Model Networks," in *Proceedings of the 20th Mediterranean Conference on Control and Automation*. Christian Doppler Laboratory for Model Based Calibration Methodologies, Vienna University of Technology, July 2012, pp. 842–847.

87. C. Hametner, C. Mayr, M. Kozek, and Jakubek, "PID Controller Design for Nonlinear Systems represented by Discrete-Time Local Model Networks ," *International Journal of Control*.

88. W. Chang, R. Hwang, and J. Hsieh, "A self-tuning PID control for a class of nonlinear systems based on the Lyapunov ...," *Journal of Process Control*, vol. 12, pp. 233–242, 2002.

89. F. Zheng, Q.-G. Wang, T. H. Lee, and X. Huang, "Robust PI controller design for nonlinear systems via fuzzy modeling approach," *IEEE Transactions on Systems, Man, and Cybernetics-Part A: Systems and Humans*, vol. 31, no. 6, pp. 666–675, 2001.

90. Z. Xiu and W. Wang, "A Novel Nonlinear PID Controller Designed By Takagi-Sugeno Fuzzy Model," *Proceedings of the 6th World Congress on Intelligent Control and Automation*, vol. 1, pp. 3724–3728, 2006.

91. K. Deb, *Multi-objective optimization using evolutionary algorithms*. Cinchester: John Wiley & Sons Ltd., 2009.

92. Z. Michalewicz, *Genetic algorithms + data structures = evolution programs*, 2nd ed. Berlin: Springer-Verlag, 1994.

93. K. Ogata, *Discrete-Time Control Systems*, 3rd ed. Prentice Hall India, 2006.

94. H. Wang, K. Tanaka, and M. Griffin, "An Approach to Fuzzy Control of Nonlinear Systems: Stability and Design Issues," *IEEE Transactions on Fuzzy Systems*, vol. 4, no. 1, pp. 14–23, 1996.

95. C. Mayr, C. Hametner, M. Kozek, and S. Jakubek, "Stability Analysis of PID Controlled Local Model Networks," in *IFAC Conference on Advances in PID Control 2012*. Christian Doppler Laboratory for Model Based Calibration Methodologies, Vienna University of Technology, Mar. 2012.

96. M. Reyes-Sierra and C. Coello, "Multi-objective Particle Swarm Optimizers: A Survey of the State-of-the-Art," *International Journal of Computational Intelligence Research*, vol. 2, no. 3, pp. 287–308, 2006.

97. L. Li, X. Yu, X. Li, and W. Guo, "A Modified PSO Algorithm for Constrained Multi-objective Optimization," in *International Conference on Network and System Security*, 2009, pp. 462–467.

98. R. Akbaria, "A multilevel evolutionary algorithm for optimizing numerical functions," *International Journal of Industrial Engineering Computations*, vol. 2, pp. 419–430, 2010.

99. K. F. Man, K.-S. Tang, and S. Kwong, *Genetic Algorithms: Concepts and Designs (Advanced Textbooks in Control and Signal Processing)*. Springer Verlag London Berlin Heidelberg, Mar. 1999.

100. PID tuning algorithm for linear plant model. [Online]. Available: http://www.mathworks.de/de/help/control/ref/pidtune.html

101. C. Guehmann and R. Malte, "Comparison of Identification Methods for Nonlinear Dynamic Systems," in *Design of Experiments (DoE) in Engine Development V: Innovative Development Methods for Vehicle Engines*, K. Röpke, Ed., 2011, pp. 290–309.

102. L. Wang and G. Feng, "Piecewise H_∞ Controller Design of Discrete Time Fuzzy Systems," *IEEE Transactions on Systems, Man, and Cybernetics, Part B: Cybernetics*, vol. 34, no. 1, pp. 682–686, 2004.

103. S. Boyd, L. El Ghaoui, E. Feron, and V. Balakrishnan, "Linear Matrix Inequalities in System and Control Theory," *SIAM Studies in Applied and Numerical Mathematics*, 1994.

104. J. R Magnus and H. Neudecker, "Matrix differential Calculus with Applications in Statistics and Econometrics," *John Wiley*, p. 395, 1999.

105. O. Foellinger, *Nichtlineare Regelung I*, 1993.

106. K. Tanaka, T. Ikeda, and H. Wang, "Fuzzy regulators and fuzzy observers: relaxed stability conditions and LMI-based designs," *IEEE Transactions on Fuzzy Systems*, vol. 6, no. 2, pp. 250–265, 1998.

107. S. P. Boyd and L. Vandenberghe, *Convex Optimization*. Cambridge Univ Press, Mar. 2004.

108. J. Löfberg, "YALMIP: a toolbox for modeling and optimization in MATLAB," *2004 IEEE International Symposium on Computer Aided Control Systems Design*, pp. 284–289, 2004.

109. YALMIP Wiki Main/What. [Online]. Available: http://users.isy.liu.se/johanl/yalmip/pmwiki.php?n=Main.What